A Concise Introduction to Cultural Anthropology

I0128609

This book offers a concise and accessible overview of cultural anthropology for those coming to the subject for the first time. It introduces key areas of the discipline and touches on its historical developments and applied aspects. As well as traditional topics such as social organization, politics, and economics, the book engages with important contemporary issues including race, gender, sexuality, and colonialism.

In a beginner-friendly format, this book is ideal for students of anthropology, as well as for the interested reader, as an introduction to the subject.

Mark Q. Sutton received his PhD in anthropology from the University of California, Riverside. He taught at California State University, Bakersfield from 1987 to 2007, where he retired as Emeritus Professor of Anthropology. He now teaches at the University of San Diego.

A Concise Introduction to Cultural Anthropology

Mark Q. Sutton

Routledge
Taylor & Francis Group

LONDON AND NEW YORK

First published 2022
by Routledge
2 Park Square, Milton Park, Abingdon, Oxon OX14 4RN

and by Routledge
605 Third Avenue, New York, NY 10158

Routledge is an imprint of the Taylor & Francis Group, an informa business

British Library Cataloguing-in-Publication Data
A catalogue record for this book is available from the British Library

Library of Congress Cataloging-in-Publication Data
Names: Sutton, Mark Q., author.
Title: A concise introduction to cultural anthropology /
Mark Q. Sutton.
Description: Abingdon, Oxon ; New York, NY : Routledge, 2021. |
Includes bibliographical references and index.
Identifiers: LCCN 2021003972 | ISBN 9780367745479 (hardback) |
ISBN 9780367745486 (paperback) | ISBN 9781003158431 (ebook)
Subjects: LCSH: Ethnology. | Ethnology–Methodology.
Classification: LCC GN316 .S976 2021 | DDC 306–dc23
LC record available at https://lccn.loc.gov/2021003972

ISBN: 978-0-367-74547-9 (hbk)
ISBN: 978-0-367-74548-6 (pbk)
ISBN: 978-1-003-15843-1 (ebk)

Typeset in Bembo
by Newgen Publishing UK

The purpose of Anthropology is to make the world safe for human differences.

Ruth Benedict

Contents

Preface

It is my experience in teaching cultural anthropology over the last 40-odd years that most students will simply not read a standard 500-page introductory textbook. Most such books contain far too much information and are simply too overwhelming (not to mention expensive). Thus, this book is intended to be a very basic "just the facts" introduction so as to make it palatable to the typical introductory student. This book is purposefully very brief with few citations and only a few specific examples so as to allow the instructor the flexibility to tailor the class and examples in the way they wish. This text has been beta tested on my last few Introduction to Cultural Anthropology classes.

Acknowledgments

I greatly appreciate the advice, comments, and suggestions of Melinda B. Sutton, Jocelyn Killmer, and the four anonymous reviewers for Routledge. I also appreciate both Katherine Ong and Alexandra McGregor at Routledge for their help and encouragement.

1 Anthropology

What is anthropology?

Anthropology is, quite literally, the study of all things related to humans and their societies throughout time and space, including their culture, language, biology, and evolution. This includes topics that are connected but not commonly associated with humans, such as monkeys, fossil animals, and nonhuman actors (e.g., spirits inhabiting nature). Humans everywhere are virtually the same, biologically (in spite of superficial but visible differences), but there are currently some 7,000 separate and distinct societies across the planet. Anthropology seeks to understand what makes these societies different, what they all have in common, and seeks to help contemporary people understand that we should embrace this great cultural diversity!

Visualize all societies on the planet as part of an orchestra. There are many sections of an orchestra: string, woodwind, brass, and percussion, each with a number and variety of instruments. Imagine each society as part of an instrument, a string on a violin or a key on a saxophone, each producing a variety of sounds. Each section, each instrument, each string or drum, each note, each tone, and each octave, all combine to produce a symphony of music. That is human culture. As societies are diminished or lost, the music of the orchestra becomes less complex and loses its beauty. Eventually, the music may fade altogether and we would have a silent world. And that would be a catastrophic loss for everyone.

Anthropology differs from other fields in that it studies all humans, everywhere, from the earliest times (millions of years ago) to today and from the Arctic to the Antarctic. No group is so small that it is not important, and no period of history or prehistory is without interest. This holistic approach has allowed anthropologists to disprove many of the generalizations that were made based only on modern or industrialized (i.e., Western societies including China and Japan), and to demonstrate some other generalizations that were not obvious once, such as the universality of complex kinship systems and dietary rules.

Anthropology is fieldwork-based, obtaining information about societies and people directly from the people themselves. Anthropologists have generally focused on nonindustrialized, traditional, or indigenous societies, many or most of which are small and largely "invisible" to Western society. More recently, however, anthropologists are working with segments of Western societies or with indigenous communities in developing nations. Anthropology is cross-cultural and comparative and seeks to understand and explain differences. The goal in this is ultimately to explain humans as a whole so as to better understand where we came from, where we are, and where we are going.

But, anthropology can also be viewed as an extension of colonialism, one in which Western interpretations are viewed as superior to those of indigenous groups. In view of this history, anthropologists are now striving to include indigenous views and interpretations into their work.

The major subfields of anthropology

The discipline of anthropology can be organized in several different ways. In the British system (Europe, Canada, and Australia), cultural anthropology is a separate field entirely, one called social anthropology. Archaeology is also a separate field with a focus on history, art, and architecture.

In the American system, anthropology is the overarching discipline and is generally divided into four major subfields (called the "four field approach"). These four major subfields are (1) biological anthropology, (2) linguistics, (3) archaeology, and (4) cultural anthropology. Depending on one's interests or focus, each of these subfields could be divided into any number of other subfields. Many of the divisions in cultural anthropology are noted below.

Biological (or physical) anthropology

The second major subdiscipline in anthropology is biological anthropology (or physical anthropology): the study of human biology through time, focusing specifically on biological evolution and human variation (e.g., Jurmain et al. 2018). Within biological anthropology are a number of specialties. Paleoanthropology is the multidisciplinary study of primate and human evolution, as well as the various aspects of geology and biology that serve as the background to such studies. The study of our closest living relatives, the nonhuman primates, is called primatology.

Biological anthropologists also specialize in human osteology, the study of the human skeleton. Because many biological anthropologists have this training, they frequently use their skills in criminal cases or major catastrophes (such as wars and airplane crashes) in which human remains are badly decomposed, fragmentary, or skeletonized.

Evolution

In its very basic definition, evolution means change, simply that: change. When most people think of evolution, they think of biological evolution: changes in gene frequency (as seen in the DNA) from generation to generation, the appearance of new species, and the extinction of other species through the process of natural selection (as seen in the fossil record). This is the definition used by biological anthropologists and biologists. Other disciplines might define evolution in different ways, but in essence, it is simply change.

But all things change and so all things evolve. As we learn new things, science evolves. As people invent new things, technology evolves. As new religions arrive, societies evolve. Even in very conservative societies, new people are born and old people die, and so the members of the society change and the society evolves. Biological and cultural evolution is constant and ongoing.

However, a common misunderstanding is that evolution has direction. It is often thought that as something evolves, it advances and gets better and that there is "progress." These notions are false. Although it is true that some things become more complex over time, not all things do and complexity itself is not necessarily an advantage. A simple amoeba living today is as "evolved" as any human being—not as complex to be sure, but certainly as evolved. It has a long evolutionary history and its continued existence reflects biological success. In the same vein, all living human societies are equally evolved, although in different environments. They are equally far from whatever society may have existed among prehistoric human ancestors. As there is no direction in evolution, there is no such thing as "devolution," there is no more or less "advanced," and there is no external scale of progress.

Anthropological linguistics

Anthropological linguistics (Ottenheimer and Pine 2018) is the study of human languages (other animals might have some sort of language but that is not considered here), including their structure (e.g., grammar, syntax, meaning, cognition) and history, since language (and so groups) can be traced back in time. Through language, people can transmit their culture from one generation to the next. This makes language the most important symbol in any society. Linguistics is considered in a bit more detail in Chapter 5.

Archaeology

Archaeology is the study of the human past (e.g., Sutton 2021a). Archaeologists want to learn the same things about past societies that cultural anthropologists do about living ones. The major differences between archaeology and cultural anthropology are in the data available and the methods used to obtain and analyze those data. Archaeologists cannot directly observe past human behavior or directly ask past people questions so they must rely on the material remains of past behaviors, as seen in their artifacts (tools), food remains, houses, human remains, settlement systems, and the like. Thus, it is difficult to obtain the entire picture of a past society.

Archaeologists, however, are able to detect change over long periods of time, can identify broad trends, and can examine transitions, such as the change of some societies from hunting and gathering to agriculture. In addition, an archaeologist can detect the traces of behavior that a cultural anthropologist might not usually see. This access to "hidden behavior" is another advantage of archaeology.

There are a number of subdivisions of archaeology. For example, prehistoric archaeology generally deals with societies prior to writing; historical archaeology is generally the archaeology on non-Native Americans in the Americas; classical archaeology studies Greece, Rome, and other Mediterranean states; Egyptology studies ancient Egypt; bioarchaeology deals with the dead; and Cultural Resource Management (CRM) is the application of archaeology in development projects. There are many more.

Cultural anthropology

Cultural anthropology is, essentially, the study of extant (living) groups with the goal of learning about, and an understanding of, the full range of human behavior. As such, there is nothing that is off limits to what a cultural anthropologist wants to know. Cultural anthropologists usually obtain their information by doing fieldwork with the society or group they are studying, perhaps for years, so as to obtain a rich and detailed knowledge of that society or group. This knowledge is then compared to information obtained by others from other societies so that comparisons can be made and a greater understanding of human behavior realized.

Other social sciences are generally different. For example, sociology tends to study industrialized societies and uses questionnaires and statistical analyses. However, there is no hard and fast rule about this division and cultural anthropologists can and do study groups, such as street gangs, in industrialized societies. Some sociologists also study traditional groups.

The study of a particular group at a particular time is called an "ethnography," and the information obtained from that study is called ethnographic data. The time period in which the group is described becomes the "ethnographic present," as the group was at that time. The comparative study of culture and societies—similarities and differences—is called ethnology. More than one ethnography is needed to do ethnology, and it is through ethnology that we can learn about culture in general, the primary goal of cultural anthropology.

Many worlds

During the Cold War between the Democratic West and Communist East, the various nation-states (e.g., those with United Nations membership) were divided into political "worlds." The First World described countries that were aligned with the United States, now commonly called "the West." The Second World was the communist states and is now sometimes called "the East." The "Third World" was the underdeveloped and unaligned states. With the end of the Cold War, the terms First and Second Worlds largely dropped from usage. However, the term "Third World" is still in common usage but now refers to developing countries.

Some anthropologists use the term "Fourth World" to classify indigenous societies without their own nations living within contemporary countries (Neely and Hume 2020). There are some 370 million Fourth World people in some 5,000 groups, speaking 4,000 languages, and living in 90 countries. Well-known examples include nearly a thousand different Native American societies in the United States and Canada and about 700 individual Indigenous Australian societies. Another Fourth World group, one that directly impacts the politics and economics of the Middle East, are the Kurds. The Kurds live mostly in Syria, Turkey, Iran, and Iraq and are striving to establish their own county, a goal resisted militarily by Turkey.

The "Fifth World" consists of past societies known mostly through archaeology (Sutton 2017). In some cases, such as Ancient Egypt or the Ancient Maya, a fair amount is known about them (but with so much still to learn). In other cases, we know of the existence of some societies and perhaps even a little bit about them. However, most past societies, perhaps tens of thousands or even hundreds of thousands of them, are completely unknown even to the point of not even knowing of their existence. The issue with this is that we cannot know the full range of human behavior if we have no knowledge of so many societies.

Perspectives on others

For the vast majority of human history, societies were small and people mostly interacted with members of their own group. Societies were almost certainly aware of one another but the lack of infrastructure, trade, and transportation provided little opportunity for interaction. As time passed, some societies became larger and more and more people had to interact with strangers, members of other societies. This interaction brought with it increasing bias, tension, distrust, and perhaps even animosity of other groups and so problems increased. Today, most people have to interact with members of other societies, many of whom are just as biased. This brings a constant and increasing challenge of dealing with strangers and having to counter the inherent bias against other societies that has dominated most of human history.

Ethnocentrism and cultural relativism

"Ethnocentrism" is the view that one's society or group is somehow better than others. All societies believe in themselves and that they are better than others, although the intensity of that belief varies. Some societies view nonmembers as not even being human. Americans tend to believe they are exceptional and are "better" than other people (as expressed in the phrase "American Exceptionalism"; e.g., Tyrre 2013). This American belief system extends to minority groups in the United States and can be easily seen in the denigration and systematic discrimination of those groups.

Every society, in varying degrees, is ethnocentric and it is a typical part of the self-identification process. The major issue with ethnocentrism is that it is often used to rationalize the mistreatment of peoples. In the history of the United States, many Americans considered Native Americans to be "savages" who were "in the way" of the expanding white "civilization." As a result, many Native people were killed, moved, or incarcerated either by the government or with their approval. Today, a number of developing Third World countries treat their indigenous people in the same way.

Anthropologists strive to mitigate ethnocentric views by taking a different approach: the suspension of judgment of other peoples' practices in order to understand them in their own cultural terms, an approach generally called "cultural relativism." In this view, all societies and people are valid and have the right to exist, to have their own culture and practices, and to speak their own language (e.g., Johansson Dahre 2017).

Placing people or societies on a pedestal as being somehow superior is also a form of ethnocentrism, a reverse ethnocentrism. We must recognize that all people are just regular people like everyone else. Everyone has strengths and weaknesses, good points and bad. We want to learn and benefit from others, not just tolerate them. Interestingly, there is no word in English for this attitude, though perhaps "open minded" is close, and that in itself tells us something.

Words matter

Western ethnocentrism is often operationalized in the words applied in reference to traditional groups. They are often called "primitive" or "savage," terms that belittle people and so can influence one's view of them. In some cases, such terms are intentionally used to dehumanize people and societies so as to justify their subjugation, cultural extermination (ethnocide), and/or their physical extermination (genocide). Treatments of many traditional groups were, and continue to be, justified in a similar manner.

But other people or societies are not primitive, weird, bad, or stupid. Instead, they are different and interesting! This amazing cultural diversity is now available to see via the Internet. Remarkably, we tend to "look down" on groups that hunt wild animals and wear animal skins, but we do the same thing and even pay a premium for our coats and upholstery made from animal skins.

Cultural appropriation

"Cultural appropriation" is the unauthorized use of customs, traits, or imagery of a society by an outsider for some purpose, generally to the detriment of the original society. For example, Native American images and icons were commonly used by American sports teams as icons or mascots. Some have argued that the use of such mascots further exploits Native Americans and that since many other mascots are animals, the use of Indians as mascots equates them with animals. By 2015, most sports teams dropped the use of Indian mascots. However, the US military continues to name many of its weapons after Native American groups or individuals, partly to convey a "warrior image" (e.g., Cheyenne, Kiowa, Apache, Blackhawk helicopters and toma-hawk missiles). In addition, the military continues to refer to enemy-occupied territory as "Indian Country." When Osama bin Laden was killed by the US military in 2011, the code word for success was Geronimo.

The New Age movement can be seen as a further exploit-ation of Native Americans by people who want to take but do not want to give back; that is, people interested in Indian cere-monies and crafts but not so much in the Indians themselves. It is interesting that beginning in 1960, when the census allowed people to declare their ethnicity, Indian populations greatly increased, perhaps partly due to "wannabe" whites declaring themselves to be Indians.

Other issues include the appropriation of traditional know-ledge to commercial purposes without the compensation of the persons or group of origin. This is true of "modern" medicines derived from indigenous knowledge, documentaries made using indigenous peoples without compensation, and even anthropologists making money from their studies without compensating their informants.

Anthropology as a science

Science can be broadly defined as learning new things, the generation of new knowledge, making order from chaos. Some scientists produce new and original data while others take existing information and look at it in a different way. Some science is experimental, doing things to see what happens. Some is conformational, testing someone else's results and supporting or rejecting them. In all of these cases, new knowledge is generated. There are two major approaches in science, empirical and nonempirical, and all societies use elements of both.

Empirical science

Empirical means objective data that are not open to interpretation; that is, data that are observable, measurable, and reproducible. Empirical science is generally based on the premise that the universe is real and measurable. For example, the weight of an item can be measured and a number generated. If someone else were to weigh the item, the result would (or should) be the same. Thus, the weight of the item is empirical. The location of a village in the landscape can be determined using GPS and so is empirical. The understanding that if you jump off a 200-ft. cliff, you will be killed is empirical. All societies understand obvious empirical reality.

Objective and subjective data

When studying a society, anthropologists gather and record a variety of information. This information includes objective data such as the location of a village, the use of specific crops, the names of local plants and animals, who is related to whom, and the like. But anthropologists also record subjective data, information that is open to interpretation, such as an opinion about something. As such, objective data are seen as "hard" and indisputable and subjective data are seen as "soft" since a different observer might interpret them in a different way.

Given that anthropology studies humans, much (but certainly not all) of the data obtained by cultural anthropologists are subjective. As such, anthropology is generally seen as a social science, one of the so-called "soft sciences" (along with sociology, psychology, philosophy, and the like). However, objective data are common in archaeology, biological anthropology, and linguistics, each of which is more of a "hard" science.

The Western scientific method

In the West (e.g., the United States, Europe), a specific method or procedure of science is followed and only certain kinds of data are acceptable. To be acceptable, data should be objective and reproducible, although in anthropology subjective data are also used. The following steps are generally followed.

1 Obtain data in the form of observations or measurements.
2 Formulate a hypothesis about the relationships between data.
3 Develop a test to judge the merit of the hypothesis. To be valid, a hypothesis must be testable. If the hypothesis is not testable, it is rejected.
4 Test the hypothesis.
5 Based on the results of the test, accept (support) or reject the hypothesis. Note that one cannot "prove" a hypothesis (proof only exists in math and courtrooms) since there is always another test that might disprove it.
6 Repeat steps 1–5.
7 A series of related hypothesis might be combined into a model, an estimation of reality.
8 Test the model.
9 Repeat steps 6 and 7 (not to mention 1–5).
10 If a hypothesis or model survives repeated testing, it may be elevated to "theory" and perhaps eventually to a "law."

The problem in science, really any science, is that its practitioners are humans. Humans make mistakes—sometimes honest ones, sometimes based on their biases. This is where constant testing, especially by scientists of other theoretical persuasions, is valuable. Thus, science is constantly being reevaluated and is, in theory, self-correcting.

Some things that are called science are not. Some are pseudoscience, data and analyses made to look scientific to a lay audience when, in fact, are not at all based on real science. Others are pure frauds and hoaxes, done for a variety of reasons, and can inhibit or set back real learning.

Finally, while all societies recognize empirical reality, not all follow the Western method of scientific inquiry. Other societies may have different methods in the development of their empirical science. Even if these other methods do not match the Western ones, they are still of interest to anthropologists.

Nonempirical science

Not all science is empirical. Recall that there are a variety of ways to learn new things and some learning is based on nonempirical information that would not be included in Western science. Some learning is based on faith or dogma, as seen in most religions. Other learning is based on personal experience, such as those gained through visions or visitations. Some societies routinely use hallucinogenic drugs to visit the realm of the supernatural and to return with knowledge obtained there. This practice is common among the traditional societies in the Amazon.

Other societies employ deprivation to maintain contact with the supernatural. For example, traditional societies on the Great Plains of North America practice a "vision quest" in which a young man will isolate himself and go without food or drink (perhaps for a week to 10 days) until he has a vision. This vision may manifest in a number of ways and often serves to guide the man later in life. Still others, such as the Indigenous Australians, use dreams, rhythmic chanting, and art to maintain contact with the supernatural world of spirits and power.

Even in Western industrial societies, nonempirical science is common. For example, many Americans believe in astrology, a practice based on one's birthdate in relation celestial objects. Others believe in palm reading, tarot cards, or psychics. None of these beliefs are based on empirical science.

Why study anthropology?

Why do we study anthropology? What are its goals and why is it relevant? A major goal is to document the range and extent of human behavior through space and time. This is a daunting task since there are literally thousands of extant societies in the world and they are all unique. In addition, there are an unknown number of past societies that we are trying to understand.

The ultimate goal of this documentation effort is to grasp what makes humans behave the way they do, how they change, and how they interact. There are some big questions to answer, such as whether the human tendency for violence and intolerance is inborn or learned. If it is learned, perhaps we can mitigate its effects and make the world a better place. Thus, anthropology strives to gain a grasp of cultural diversity and an appreciation for that diversity. It is also to illustrate that diversity is a strength and not a weakness.

To understand where we are going, we need to understand where we are and where we have been. It is like being a passenger in a car driving along a highway. Are you happy just being in the car? Where have you been in the car? Home? A restaurant? A motel? Any fond memories? Who are you with? Who is driving? Where are you going? Are you paying attention to the cars next to you? Worried about one crashing into you? Do you care? Are you just oblivious to your situation and surroundings? Few people would be that disinterested on their car trip. Anthropology is the field that asks all these questions about the journey of humankind.

Anthropology seeks to increase our understanding of ourselves, to develop an appreciation for other societies and practices, to learn useful things, such as management techniques, technology, and medicine, from other societies. In addition, anthropology endeavors to help preserve endangered societies (past and present) so that their culture is not lost.

Lastly, in a very practical sense, anthropological knowledge may be applied to real world issues (see Chapter 13). Anthropologists attempt to help societies under stress, to assist them if they are impacted by development, to help preserve their territories, and to represent them in the legal system. In addition, if Western societies want to do business with other societies, an understanding of their customs and traditions is necessary. Also, the military needs similar information so as to successfully carry out their missions.

Anthropology is also relevant to the political and social stresses currently gripping the United States (see Ackermann et al. 2019). It is very important to learn about things like white supremacy, the movements for social and racial justice, such as #MeToo, Black Lives Matter, LGBTQ rights, the feminist movement, police brutality, political discord, racial disparities in health and the response to the Covid-19 pandemic (e.g., Goodman 2016), and a host of other issues. Anthropology is uniquely positioned to contribute to understanding these concerns.

Chapter summary

Anthropology is the study of all aspects of humans through space and time. The four major subfields of anthropology are biological anthropology (the study of the biology and evolution of humans and other primates), anthropological linguistics (the study of human language), archaeology (the study of past societies), and cultural anthropology (the study of extant societies). Anthropologists study a wide variety of groups, including small traditional societies, communities in developing countries, marginalized segments of populations, and others.

Anthropology is an empirical science and follows the Western scientific method. However, nonempirical science is recognized as existing and worthy of study and understanding.

Anthropology takes the position that all people and societies are valid and valued and must not be judged. Anthropology strives to overcome issues such as ethnocentrism—the intolerance of others. The goal is to learn about, and so understand human behavior and apply those lessons to contemporary problems. One needs to know where they have been and where they are now to understand where they are going.

2 A very short history of cultural anthropology

Anthropology is a new discipline, having been formalized in the latter half of the 1800s. A number of other disciplines developed at about the same time, mostly due to the same basic forces. Before approximately 1860, the teachings of the Church dominated thought, finally to be surpassed by a belief in empirical science. But this was not an easy or rapid transition.

On the development of Western scientific thought

A number of events combined to create the conditions for the development of Western scientific thought (other regions, such as China, had a sophisticated science at the time but did not generally influence the West). First, the invention of the printing press in 1446 made the production of books far less expensive (before the printing press, books were hand written and extremely expensive) meaning that many more people had access to knowledge and literacy greatly increased.

Second, in 1453, the Ottomans conquered Constantinople (now Istanbul, Turkey), the seat of the Orthodox Christian Church and a center of knowledge and learning. Once the Ottomans entered, many academic people fled to Western Europe and the "center" of knowledge shifted west.

Finally, the European invasion of the New World in 1492 (the second European incursion since the Norse [aka Vikings] had first arrived in about A.D. 1000) resulted in the need for explanations of the myriad of new people and lands encountered. The European colonial powers (England, France, Belgium, the Netherlands, Spain, and Portugal) claimed large swaths of the planet and subjugated uncounted traditional societies. As a result, a great deal of information about these societies flooded Europe. Although religious explanations continued to dominate European thought, people began asking questions.

In the early 1800s, the age of the earth was put (by the Church) at about 6,000 years (it had been deduced that creation took place at 9 am on October 23, 4004 B.C). In the 1830s, Charles Lyell formulated the Principle of Uniformitarianism, arguing that the same basic geological processes operating now (erosion, deposition, volcanism, and the like) have always operated in the same manner. Thus, Lyell argued, the earth must be millions of years old to account for the visible geology (we now know Earth is about 4.5 billion years old).

At about the same time, stone tools were found beneath extinct animals in France, meaning (following the Law of Superposition) that the stone tools must be older than the extinct animals. Then, in 1848, extinct humans, the Neanderthals, were discovered. These finds indicated that extinct humans and extinct animals coexisted in a time prior to the accepted date of creation, calling into question the Church dogma on the origins of people.

A natural evolution

In the mid-1800s, the dominant cosmology in Western Europe was creationism, as articulated by Christianity. In that cosmology, white people were descended from Adam and Eve while people of other colors had "degenerated" (punished by God?). At that time, the belief was that things had remained unchanged from the creation (which, of course, ignored the degeneration thesis) so it was claimed that there was no evidence of evolution. This view was reinforced by the inability of anyone to explain how evolution might have occurred in nature. Attempts at such an explanation had been made, such as the doctrine of acquired characteristics (e.g., giraffe necks became long due to their reaching higher and higher for leaves in trees), but none of the explanations made sense. Although people had been altering species for farming purposes (directed evolution) for 10,000 years, no one could explain a mechanism of natural evolution, and so creationism remained dominant.

However, in 1859, Charles Darwin published "On the Origin of the Species" and proposed a mechanism for natural evolution that made sense. In the 1830s, Darwin had served as a naturalist on the British ship HMS *Beagle* and had conducted extensive studies on a number of natural systems, particularly on the Galapagos Islands off Ecuador. Once back in England, he began working on his theory, only published in 1859 because another scientist (Alfred Wallace) had independently arrived at the same conclusion, forcing Darwin to publish.

Despite considerable effort by the Church, Darwin's ideas could not be refuted and his theory of natural selection became generally accepted (but there are some who still do not accept it, even today). This resulted in a gradual shift from supernatural explanations to natural ones; that is, a shift from religion to science. This accelerated the development of scientific disciplines within universities.

The emergence of anthropology as a discipline

Anthropology emerged as a formal discipline during the height of European colonialism, a time when a great deal of raw information about subjugated traditional peoples and their societies began to flood into colonial powers, especially Great Britain. Much of this information was in the form of military records, explorer accounts and diaries, missionary records, questionnaires, and the like. Most of this information was just filed and not really examined in any detail.

However, some interested people did look at those records and began to get a picture of what people were where, their general descriptions, customs, beliefs and their social, political, and economic systems. One of these people was Edward B. Tylor, working in London with British records. Tylor began corresponding with an American, Lewis Henry Morgan, who was studying Native Americans. Tylor had never really worked directly with traditional people while Morgan had. Together, they developed a theory of how societies developed; the first coherent theory in anthropology.

Morgan was an attorney and in the 1840s, was hired by the Haudenosaunee Iroquois for a land case. Morgan became fascinated by Iroquois culture, and in 1851, he published the "League of the Ho-dé-no-sau-nee, Iroquois," the first ethnography ever published in anthropology. This classic work (Morgan 1851) is still in print and remains a standard reference on the Haudenosaunee (as they were in 1851). This work had a huge impact, both on anthropology (it set a standard for future work) and on the Haudenosaunee, who became quite famous as a result. Morgan went on to greater accomplishments in anthropology, including the theory of Unilinear Cultural Evolution and in the classification of kinship systems, many of which were named after North American Indian groups, and is still in use today.

Unilinear cultural evolution

Both Tylor and Morgan were doing some anthropology in the 1850s but most of this work was in compiling records and searching for common trends. After the publication of Darwin's work on evolution (Darwin 1859), Tylor and Morgan both thought that human societies would also have evolved. Using the information Tylor had gathered from government records and information obtained first-hand by Morgan, the two men collaborated on a theory called Unilinear Cultural Evolution (UCE). UCE proposed that societies evolved up a single line (unilinear), beginning at the bottom of the scale and striving to "climb the ladder" to eventually become like Europeans (Table 2.1).

The problems with UCE are numerous, serious, and fatal. To begin with, Tylor and Morgan misunderstood the basic concept of evolution (still widely misunderstood even today), that there is no set direction in evolution and there is no such thing as "progress." Thus, there cannot be any evolution "up" a line toward a goal. Next, the model was based on very few actual data. Further, they arbitrarily employed only technological criteria

Table 2.1 Simplified stages of unilinear cultural evolution by Tylor and Morgan

Stage	Criteria	Example culture
Civilization	Writing	"Modern" Europeans
Upper Barbarian	Use of iron	Early Greeks
Middle Barbarian	Agriculture	Hopi
Lower Barbarian	Pottery	Iroquois
Upper Savagery	Bow and arrow	Polynesians
Middle Savagery	Fire and speech	Indigenous Australians
Lower Savagery	Before fire and speech	No living examples

Source: Table by author.

(something cherished by Westerners) in their classification and thus ignored the many other aspects of culture. For example, the Indigenous Australians are listed at the bottom since they have the least complex technology. However, if kinship complexity were the criterion, the Indigenous Australians would be on top and Europeans would be at the bottom.

In addition, UCE was very ethnocentric and unfortunately formalized the use of "savage" and "barbarian" in reference to traditional societies. These terms are still in use today and have been institutionalized by governments to justify oppression and even the ethnocide or genocide of some groups. In popular culture, and sometimes even in anthropology, savage generally came to mean hunter-gatherers, barbarian to mean pastoralists, and civilized to mean farmers.

Nevertheless, UCE was the first great theory in anthropology, used a scientific approach, and was of considerable importance since it gave subsequent researchers something to scrutinize. In addition, irrespective of its scientific merit, UCE considered all societies to be natural and ordinary, much better than the previous view of degeneration and punishment. A similar unilinear view of cultural development was (is) held by Marxist theory that held advanced communism to be the pinnacle of development.

Historical particularism

Franz Boas was a German with a PhD in physics. In the 1870s, there was so little literature on any scientific field that most scientists, including Boas, had read the UCE ideas of Tylor and Morgan. Not having any detailed anthropological knowledge, he did not question it. However, on an expedition to the Arctic in 1883, Boas realized that the Inuit he encountered were very well adapted to their environment and that the evolutionary ideas embodied in UCE were false. He argued that each society was the product of their own history and adaptation to their particular environment. This school of thought became known as "Historical Particularism" and soon replaced UCE as the dominant theory in anthropology. It remains important even today.

Boas further believed that each society was valid and should not be judged by others (cultural relativism) and that race was not a factor in human development. These ideas remain pillars in anthropology. Finally, Boas introduced the scientific method to anthropology and argued that many more detailed data were necessary to make generalizations and that intensive detailed ethnographic work was needed.

Boas is viewed as "the father of American anthropology." Boas developed the first PhD program in anthropology and trained the first wave of anthropologists that would go on to establish departments of anthropology at other universities with their students doing the same again. Boas and his students, and then their students, amassed huge quantities of information, a great deal of which still remains to be analyzed. Much of this effort focused on Western North America, as native groups in the West had survived intact longer than those in the East, where many had been long extinct before any anthropological work could be done.

Functional/structuralism

Functionalism is the idea that the key questions in anthropology centered on the function of institutions in a society. Others believed that it was the structure of social institutions that was the key to understanding. Before long, it was realized that these two approaches were asking very similar questions and so are now generally combined.

A proponent of functionalism, Bronislaw Malinowski was in Australia when World War One began. He was technically a German citizen (and so an enemy alien) and was to be interned but he persuaded the Australians to allow him to work in Trobriand Islands north of Australia for the duration of the war. Malinowski, in daily contact with the Trobriand Islanders for four years, discovered the advantages of such close observation and participation and developed the "participant observation" field method, still the primary approach in anthropology.

Another major contribution was made by Margaret Mead, a student of Boas, who went to Samoa in 1925 to do fieldwork on sex (a woman doing that in the 1920s was itself controversial). Her works, "Coming of Age in Samoa" (1928) and her later "Sex and Temperament in Three Primitive Societies" (1935) remain important contributions to the study of sex in traditional societies. Mead became an important figure in the feminist movement, in women's rights, and in the sexual revolution.

Ruth Benedict pioneered the study of the personalities of societies. She worked with the Puebloan people of the American Southwest and conducted a study on the national character (personality) on the Japanese during World War Two. The conclusion of her study on Japanese personality, "The Chrysanthemum and the Sword" (1946), were later found to be erroneous, highlighting the dangers of doing studies of people at a distance. Benedict is also known for noting that "the purpose of anthropology is to make the world safe for human differences."

Diffusionism

In the early 1900s, the idea that many cultural traits had diffused into societies from a central place became popular. This became an easy and convenient way to explain particular phenomena, and many anthropologists believed that diffusion was the prime instrument of change. Early diffusionists argued that complex societies developed in only one or two central places, such as ancient Egypt, and then spread to all of the other locations where other complex societies later emerged. Subsequent research has demonstrated that this was not always the case, so diffusion is no longer an automatic explanation for the distribution of cultural traits.

Multilinear cultural evolution

Despite the failure of UCE, it is clear that culture and societies do change through time and that there must be some way to deal with cultural evolution. Thus, the idea that societies evolved, not up a single line, but along many lines (depending on conditions) became known as Multilinear Cultural Evolution (MCE). While it is known that some societies have changed very slowly and others have changed rapidly, it is not understood how and why this happens and so it remains an important research topic.

Cultural ecology

For a time in the mid-twentieth century, anthropologists believed that environment was the major factor in cultural development (called environmental determinism) but it soon became apparent that culture itself was the primary factor in cultural evolution. The complex interaction between culture and environment is now the field of Human or Cultural Ecology and includes a variety of research approaches (Sutton and Anderson 2014, also see Chapter 12).

Cultural materialism

Cultural materialism is the idea that societies are organized to address practical problems. This is a very basic approach that centers on technology, economy (e.g., food), environment, and population. This method begins with the idea that cultural institutions can be explained by direct material payoff. To explain some cultural phenomenon, the researcher begins by looking for a specific direct material payoff, such as food. If the first payoff alone proves inadequate as an explanation, another material payoff, such as shelter, is considered and perhaps added to the first. If all material payoffs are eliminated or are inadequate as explanations, then research would move outside the realm of direct material payoffs and investigate psychological or sociological factors.

Postmodernism

Beginning in the 1980s, some became dissatisfied with science and the modern world in general. These "postmodernists" were critical of all things modern and argued that science itself was flawed. Postmodernism generally took a very subjective and antiscientific stance in opposition to the objectivism of science. Some argued that because anthropologists themselves were biased, any interpretations they made were subjective and that there was no single truth. It was also argued that anthropology was an "agent of colonialism" and viewed other societies from a narrow, capitalist, male, Western perspective, ignoring the viewpoints of the traditional people themselves. Many view postmodernism as a shift away from an unemotional anthropology and toward a more humanistic and democratic anthropology that recognizes and embraces issues of inequality, domination, gender, minorities, and the voices of the underrepresented.

Some of the underlying arguments of postmodernism are difficult to accept. For example, the contention that science is dehumanizing and cannot be used to analyze humans implies that humans are above nature and so somehow above analysis. Yet, after declaring that people cannot be analyzed, postmodernists proceed to analyze them. They suggest that all interpretations are equal and valid, but then reject some in favor of others.

The postmodern approach seems to be a collection of new perspectives added on to existing theory rather than an entirely new theoretical paradigm. In that sense, these new approaches are not technically "postmodern" but are perspectives just recently added. In the end, it seems that postmodernism has engaged anthropologists to include issues of social stratification, minorities, gender, suppressed peoples, ideologies, and the like, and this is a positive development.

Chapter summary

Anthropology is but one of the sciences developed in Europe within the last 500 years (some other sciences are older). Beginning in the mid-1400s, literacy increased, knowledge became more varied and widespread, and universities developed. When Europeans encountered the New World in 1492, there began a period of colonization and exposure to a myriad of different people and societies, creating a need for the colonizing powers to somehow deal with those societies (which they did in different ways). The 1859 publication of a workable method of natural evolution considerably increased the dominance of science in European societies.

The first coherent theory in cultural anthropology was UCE which was very ethnocentric and embodied a basic misunderstanding of evolution in general. This theory was replaced by Historical Particularism which held that societies were the product of their particular history and environment.

Other theoretical approaches were developed, such as Functionalism (how institutions functioned), Structuralism (how institutions were structured), diffusion, MCE, Cultural Ecology, and Materialism. In the 1980s, a variety of other research approaches and issues, mostly under the umbrella of postmodernism, were added. These include gender, inequality, social stratification, minorities, and suppressed peoples. All this makes cultural anthropology very dynamic.

3 Culture, personality, and worldview

What is culture?

Simply put, culture is learned and shared behavior in humans. All animals, and even some plants, also have learned and shared behaviors but here we only consider humans. Humans have only minimal instincts, such as self-preservation, reproduction, and being maternal. Thus, virtually all of human behavior is learned: what one likes, how one thinks, what language one speaks, one's beliefs, one's values, one's biases, what is good to eat, how one views the world, and so on. All of these traits are socially transmitted, learned from other members of one's society. Everything one experiences is filtered through the lens of their cultural background. It forms the basis for the generation of appropriate behavior, which is defined by the society. In essence, then, culture is integrated into all social systems and forms one's view of reality.

There are a large number of traits that all human societies possess, called "cultural universals." For example, all societies have some form of political organization, social structure, kinship organization, economic system, religious system, and marriage. While the general categories of such systems are universal, the details vary greatly from society to society.

Culture is transmitted using symbols, signs, emblems, and/or other things that represent something in a meaningful way. Probably the most important of the symbols is language, the mechanism by which humans transmit culture from one generation to another, mostly through oral tradition. Before written language, visual symbols were the primary method of communicating status, power, and prestige. Look around you, symbols with meaning are visible everywhere.

Culture forms an incredibly flexible adaptive mechanism that other animals lack. Humans do not readily adapt biologically; if we get cold, we do not grow fur, we put on someone else's. People make extensive use of technology and that permits us to do a great many things. Technology is so important to us that we Westerners tend to judge other societies on their technological complexity. Using culture and technology, we humans have been able to occupy almost the entire land surface of the planet, across many diverse environments from the Arctic to the Amazon.

Of course, culture can also be maladaptive. If a society makes enough bad decisions, such as exploiting too much of their resource base, or engaging in warfare with a superior enemy, or exhausting their agricultural fields, they could simply disappear. In that case, they would become one of the societies of the Fifth World.

What is a society?

While culture is learned behavior in general, a "society" is a group of people who share a specific set of learned behaviors that is different from other groups (the term "a culture" is often used to mean a society but this can be confusing and so we will use the term society). Most societies are small and identify themselves by having their own language, religion, philosophy, morality and ethics, kinship system, regulated reproductive pool, dress, food and cuisine, and the like. In addition, each society defines what it considers to be acceptable behavior. Although some traits may be shared with other societies (e.g., English is spoken in several different societies), each society has a distinctive suite of traits that makes it unique. Thus, most small societies have a fixed set of traits shared by all its members, traits that identify their ethnicity.

In larger societies, the constellation of shared traits may be much more variable, such as having a number of languages, different kinds of food, different geographic origins of its members, several religions, and a more expansive view of acceptable behavior. This diversity of traits is what separates independent self-contained societies from larger, multicultural, societies. Not all traits are good ones. In the United States, for example, the mistreatment of minorities has become "normalized" to some degree. The Black Lives Matter movement, detention of immigrant children, and other protests are in response to such violence. South Africa went through a similar process that eventually ended apartheid.

Functions of a society

Why do societies exist and what they do? Among the functions of a society is to provide an identity to its members; a group identity that sets one's group as separate from others. There are a number of reasons that this is important. First, it is necessary to be able to identify members of one's group so as to provide a social structure for reproduction and mutual support. The shared culture of a society then provides the basis for "enculturation": the socialization and training of the young.

Next, a group identify is necessary to have a common approach for the production and distribution of goods and services within the group. It also serves to facilitate social interaction and provide ways to avoid or resolve conflicts, both within the society and with other societies. A society is also needed to meet the psychological and emotional needs of its members.

Personality

Personality is the distinctive way a person thinks, feels, and behaves. While this is influenced to some degree by genetics, much of it is learned. As children are enculturated, each individual is indoctrinated to the society's collective views of acceptable behavior, logic systems, and the like. Thus, one's personality is typically a reflection of a person's learned understanding of the societies' expectations of behavior.

The personality of a society as a whole is effectively the "average" of the personalities of its members, each of whom was first enculturated by the society. This circular process can result in stability and homogeneity, especially in a small society. However, the larger and more complex a society becomes, the more diverse its personality may become and so we speak of cultural personality in a broad sense. But because each individual is different, the personality of a society will change (evolve) over time. In some cases, the influence of a single significant individual could dramatically alter the personality of a society. The anthropological study of the personality of a society can be quite difficult, especially if done at a distance (recall Ruth Benedict's study of Japanese National Personality during World War Two).

Perception and cognition

How do we make sense of what we see or hear and how do we interpret it? "Perception" is the ability to acquire information from ones surroundings through a number of mechanisms, including sight (visual acuity and color vision), sound (range of tone), smell and taste (both with important genetic variations), and touch (sensitivity). Every individual has different perceptive capacities and even if two people experience exactly the same stimuli, they will not register it in precisely the same way. Thus, everyone perceives the world differently, even if only slightly.

"Cognition" is the interpretation of the data collected through perception. Even if two people receive the same data through perception, each will process the data through their own cultural lens and the interpretive results might be strikingly different. Thus, your biology (and technology) determines your perception while your culture (enculturation) largely determines your interpretation. Any interpretation of data is dependent on your personality, your logic system, and your ethnocentrism—combined to form your worldview.

Elements of personality

Each society (and person) has a unique set of ways it views the world and its place in it. While every society is ethnocentric, the degree of ethnocentrism varies. For example, "morality" is an understanding of the difference between good and evil while "ethics" is an understanding (and practice) of right and wrong based on morality. Consider the killing of another person: when is it immoral or unethical? A very ethnocentric society might view nonmembers as nonhuman so most any behavior toward them, even killing them, might be perfectly moral. A less ethnocentric society may consider violence toward anyone to be unethical. Is killing an enemy in warfare unethical? Is sacrificing a member of your own society on the basis of religious belief immoral? Is the enslavement of other humans ethical? The Romans had no problem with slavery and although the Americans ended the practice, they continue to struggle with its ethics and aftermath. All of these questions are decided by each society.

Each society (and person) thinks in a particular way based on their own rules of logic. The use of different classification systems can illustrate different logic systems (anyone looking for something in a grocery store knows this). In Western societies, animals are classified by anatomy, such as their similarities in skeletal structure, whether they are warm blooded or not, and whether they nurse their young. In this system, a deer living in the mountains and a seal in the ocean are both classified as mammals—a logical system. But consider a system based on habitat and not on anatomy. In this latter system, both fish and seals would be grouped together as marine animals while deer would be very different—a terrestrial animal. This too is a logical system.

Many other elements of personality could be described, such as concepts of privacy and modesty, expressions of love or affection, attitudes toward sexual relationships, treatment of women, methods of disciplining children, aggression, independence, and many more. There is a great deal of variation.

Of additional interest are concepts of time. Western societies tend to measure time precisely (monotemporal), such as when your Introduction to Cultural Anthropology class begins and ends. Some other societies have a more general concept of time (polytemporal), meaning things happen in a more leisurely manner. Amusingly, with all the temporal precision that is characteristic of Western societies, the calendar used in the United

States (and many other places), is not very precise, as can be seen by the necessity of having to add an extra day every four years (leap year). The Maya calendar is much more precise.

What is "acceptable"?

Each society defines what kinds of behavior is acceptable. In some societies, the range of such behavior is quite narrow while in others, such as in the United States, there is much greater latitude. Thus, what is acceptable in one society may not be in another, as they all vary. As society evolves, as attitudes change, as individuals enter and leave the society, the definition of "acceptable" evolves. For example, gay marriage or pot smoking, once viewed as unacceptable and even illegal in US society, are both now largely ordinary.

Each society will decide how to maintain acceptable behavior. First, such behavior must be made desirable (a task of enculturation) and second, there must be some sanction (penalty) for deviation. Unwanted behavior can be divided into three categories. "Folkways" are minor and informal rules that if violated, will result in minor sanctions, such as an expression of displeasure. "Mores" are informal but important rules that if violated, can result in sanctions such as being ostracized from the group. "Laws" are formal rules that if violated, can result in serious sanctions such as fines, incarceration, or even death (execution). If a person consistently operates outside the acceptable limits of their society, they may even be classified as deviant or mentally ill.

Worldview

"Worldview," a cultural universal, is the distinctive way in which an individual, or a society, views the world and its place in it. Worldview includes an understanding of how the universe works and of cosmology, the explanation of the origin of things. Ethnocentrism is an obvious influence on worldview as most societies view themselves as being at the center of their universe.

Cosmology

Cosmology is the explanation of the universe: the creation of the world, the origin of the things in the world, and how people came to be. Each society has a cosmology, usually encoded in religion. Some societies have more than one cosmology. In Western societies, many people continue to subscribe to religious cosmologies, such as the Christian belief in the creation of the world by God during a six-day time period. But there is another cosmology in Western societies; a scientific and natural one in which the "big bang" is the origin of the universe.

It is often the case that many of the activities that formed the world happened in an earlier time, a noncalendric time when people were animals and animals were people. Most societies have such concepts.

A well-known example of this is the Dreamtime of the Indigenous Australians. During the Dreamtime, the creator/god, Rainbow Serpent, created land from the mud at the bottom of the ocean and the animal/people came into being. These animal/people beings were not gods but inhabitants of the Dreamtime world. The actions of these beings created the world as was later known, such as the movements of Crocodile's tail forming a river valley or Kangaroo being frozen in place forming a mountain range. Thus, all things in the current (calendric) world can be explained by what happened in the Dreamtime, the exception being Europeans and their behavior, something that could never be properly explained.

However, in order for the world to continue to function, the sacred places of the Dreamtime must be ritually maintained. Certain places are very special, contain power, and contain images of the Dreamtime (Figure 3.1). Certain people are responsible for the maintenance of those places and for the landscape in general. Failure to properly maintain these places could result in catastrophe. People may suffer illness and the land would cease to provide the resources necessary for human life.

Figure 3.1 Images of the Dreamtime at a sacred place in Australia (photo by Markus Vaeth, FreeImages.com).

Chapter summary

Culture is learned behavior in humans. A society is a group of people that share specific set of cultural traits, such as language and religion, different than other groups. Societies function to give an identity to its members and to provide a structure for reproduction, enculturation, interaction, conflict resolution, and the like.

Most small societies are homogeneous but in larger societies there may be distinct ethnic groups, communities that identify themselves based on various cultural features such as shared ancestry and common origin, language, customs, and traditional beliefs. Societies may also contain subcultures, relatively small groups with distinctive variations of, and within, the primary society.

Personality is the distinctive way a person thinks, feels, and behaves, based mostly on one's enculturation. The personality of a society as a whole is effectively the "average" of the personalities of its members and will change (evolve) over time. The way one interprets the world depends on perception—the ability to take in information from one's surroundings. The interpretations of those data are dependent on one's cognition, itself dependent on one's biology and culture.

Personality includes concepts of morality and ethics, systems of logic, classificatory systems, privacy and modesty, expressions of love or affection, attitudes toward sexual relationships, treatment of women, methods of disciplining children, aggression, independence, concepts of time, and many more.

Each society defines acceptable behavior and how such behavior can be enforced. Folkways are minor and informal rules; mores are informal but important rules, while laws are quite formal rules. If a person consistently operates outside the limits imposed by their society, they may be classified as deviant or mentally ill.

Worldview is the distinctive way in which an individual, or a society, views the world and includes an understanding of how the universe works and of cosmology, the explanation of the origin of things. Cosmology is the explanation of the universe, the creation of the world, the origin of the things in the world, and how people came to be. Each society has a cosmology, usually encoded in religion, and some societies have more than one.

4 Doing cultural anthropology

Cultural anthropology is essentially the study of extant (living) societies. What do cultural anthropologists want to know? Everything!! One would want to describe the society and record information on the basics of any society such as social structure, political system, economic system, religion, and so forth. One could ask how well the society satisfies the biological, social, and psychological needs of its members. Is the society stable? What is the domestic life like? What is the physical and mental health of the population? What is their nutritional status? What is their demographic structure? What is the incidence of violence, crime, and delinquency? We want to know everything.

Anthropological methods

There are several ways to do cultural anthropological research, including library research, using questionnaires, or doing actual fieldwork. Library research involves compiling the available information on a society, such as a previous ethnography, and perhaps other societies (other ethnographies), to make new interpretive connections and learn new things (doing ethnology). Questionnaires could be used to augment the library data. Or, one could conduct original field research to generate new data. The results of any fieldwork would then be compared to earlier studies (ethnology) and so still require library research.

Whatever method or combination of methods used, it is likely that both objective and subjective the data would have been obtained. Each data set would be analyzed using different techniques, such as statistics.

Fieldwork

A great deal of anthropological research involves direct contact with, and observation of, members of the society being studied. Depending on the circumstances, such contact might be brief, involve interviews and/or questionnaires, and might be repeated often. In other cases, the contact and observation of a group may be sustained for weeks, or months, or even years at a time. This method is called participant observation, a technique pioneered by Malinowski.

Participant observation

In participant observation, the anthropologist lives with a group for extended times, perhaps supplemented by interviews and questionnaires. To be able to communicate, the anthropologist must learn the language of the group, be accepted (as well as possible), participate in the activities of the group, collect genealogies and life histories, and record as many data as possible. All of this is done under the auspices of cultural relativism and none of this is easy.

Cultural anthropologists working directly with people have a number of ethical obligations. The most important obligation is always to the people being studied. There must be informed consent and the studied group must approve the study in advance. The anthropologist must publish their results and if there is any financial gain (e.g., a patent on a new medicine), the groups must share in the rewards. In all cases, the studied group must be treated with respect and should be kept informed about the progress of the work and provided a copy of any publications.

Preparation for fieldwork

The preparation for fieldwork involves a number of steps. First, one has to decide what group they want to study. Next, permission to do the research has to be granted by both the government of the host nation-state and by the group in question. It is best to learn the local language prior to going into the field but this may be impractical if the language is not well-known. Finally, one has to secure funding for the research, such as money for transportation, supplies, extra personnel (e.g., a camera operator), support to analyze the data once back home, and publication costs. This part of the process can take considerable time and effort.

Once in the field

Ethnographic field research can be difficult. Once in the field, one must face personal challenges while trying to adjust to a new society. Among the numerous mental challenges that anthropologists commonly face are the struggle to be accepted by the group being studied, culture shock, loneliness, feeling like an ignorant outsider, being socially awkward in a new cultural setting, and struggling with one's inherent ethnocentrism. At the same time, one must identify key consultants, collect various types of data, do mapping, do any needed photography and filming, and record everything.

One also has to understand that some people might resent being studied and may provide knowingly false information (i.e., lie) about their society. There will also be behavior that is hidden from outsiders for a variety of reasons, such as religious prohibitions, embarrassment, or behavior considered unacceptable. Finally, there will be rules that people are supposed to follow and they will claim that they do. But in real life, they may not. For example, it is against the law to exceed the speed limit on a highway and so not speeding is the "ideal behavior." But the "actual behavior" is that many people speed (and can get a ticket if caught).

There is always an inherent bias in all fieldwork. One such bias is sex and until the 1980s or so, most fieldwork was done by males. After that, the participation of female anthropologists became much more common, the result of feminist anthropology (e.g., Lewin and Silverstein 2016). Another bias is age, such as an older anthropologist not being able to connect with children. Also remember that the society being studied also has biases against the researcher.

Finally, anthropological fieldwork will always impact the society under study. Their typical behavior will be altered by the presence of an anthropologist, meaning the record of their behavior will always be a bit biased. The society and its members will be exposed to new ideas and technologies, become part of a larger world, perhaps be exposed to new diseases, and come under greater pressure from the "outside" world.

After fieldwork

After the fieldwork is completed and the ethnographic information collected, the next challenge is to compile it together in a way that accurately describes the society. Written ethnographies are more traditional but certainly not the only method to document the data. Sometimes ethnographic research is documented with sound recordings, photography, and videos in addition to writing.

The results of the study might be published in a book, as a series of articles in journals, or both. In addition to the information about the studied group, there would be an effort to compare the data to other groups, that is, to do some ethnology. This work would set the stage for future studies.

Differing viewpoints

One of the weaknesses in the study of other people is that the observer is usually from another society, an outsider. Thus, the researcher is influenced by his or her own society when evaluating another. This is called the "etic" view. Anthropologists recognize this and try to compensate for it by being as objective as possible, and can often see things that members of the society cannot. When a person studies his or her own society, an insider looking at the inside, it is called the "emic" view. Such a study is also biased since the observer has no other perspective. A more complete understanding of another society can be obtained by combining both emic and etic views. Although these two views need not be in agreement, since diversity of opinion is itself interesting and informative, it is possible for one view to inform the other.

Chapter summary

Cultural anthropology is the study of extant (living) societies and cultural anthropologists want to know everything! Cultural anthropological research is done using library research, questionnaires, interviews, and/or actual fieldwork. Fieldwork is generally participant observation in which the anthropologist lives with a group for an extended time.

The preparation for fieldwork involves deciding which group to study, obtaining permissions, learning the local language, and securing funding. In addition, there are a number of ethical obligations, the most important of which is to the people being studied. There must be informed consent, the anthropologist must publish their results, and any financial gain must be shared.

Once in the field, there are many challenges such as the struggle to be accepted by the group being studied, culture shock, and struggling with one's inherent ethnocentrism. At the same time, one must do the work. In some cases, people will lie or mislead, say one thing and do another, and hide certain behaviors. One also has to deal with the inherent bias in all fieldwork, such as sex and age.

After fieldwork, the data must be analyzed and conclusions written. The results might be published in a book and/or articles. In addition, there would be an effort to compare the data to other groups, that is, to do some ethnology.

There are always differing viewpoints: the etic view is that of an outsider of a subject group; that is, the view of the anthropologist of the studied group. The emic view is that of the insider of themselves. Both views are biased and both should be considered in any analysis.

5 Anthropological linguistics

Linguistics is the systematic study of all aspects of language while anthropological linguistics focuses on human language (Ottenheimer and Pine 2018). A language is a system of communication using sounds, gestures, or marks that are put together in accordance to a specific set of rules resulting in meanings that are intelligible to all who share that language. Through language, people transmit their culture from one generation to the next. Thus, language is the most important symbol in any society. Anthropological linguistics can be divided into three major categories: descriptive, historical, and social.

Today, there are, perhaps, 7,000 languages still spoken worldwide, including American Sign Language (ASL) and other sign languages. However, most people on the planet speak 1 of only 20 or so languages. As small societies are absorbed by larger ones, their languages are spoken by fewer and fewer people, now mostly elders. Today, some languages are spoken by fewer than five people. Although there are some programs to preserve languages, the number of spoken languages is rapidly declining.

Why should we all worry about this? First, recall that language is the way in which culture is transmitted from one generation to the next. The loss of a language means that the culture of that society cannot be transmitted to the next generation and so the society itself may be lost.

Second, people think in their language. Given that languages differ, the thinking that derives from it must also differ; a model called "cognitive linguistics." One's thoughts, worldview, morality, philosophy, and the like would be shaped and limited by one's language. Thus, the loss of a language means the loss of a unique way of thinking and of human understanding.

Descriptive linguistics

To understand a language, one much first describe it and understand its structure, the task of descriptive linguistics. Each language has a set of formal rules, "grammar," which governs the entire structure of a language, including the arrangement of clauses, phrases, and words in sentences and paragraphs. The major elements of grammar include morphology and syntax.

"Morphology" in linguistics is the rules of word formation in a language, that is, how words are put together. "Phonemes" are distinct units of sound while "morphemes" are the smallest units of sound that carry a meaning. "Syntax" is the set of rules regarding the production of phrases and sentences. "Phonology" is the study of the production, transmission, and reception of speech sounds. The number of phonemes used varies by language, and range between 161 and 11. English uses 42. Many languages use "clicks" but such phonemes are not used in English.

Roughly 70% of the world's languages are "tonal languages," where the pitch of a spoken word is an essential part of its pronunciation and meaning. English is a nontonal language, and although tones in English can convey an attitude or indicate a question, they do not change the meaning of words. In Mandarin, the careless use of tones with the syllable "ma" could cause one to call someone's mother a horse!

Once the structure of a language is understood, it is classified in relation to other languages. This can be done in a number of ways but a common approach is phylogenetic (like a family tree), based on word comparisons. In that system, the largest division is the phylum, followed by superfamily, family, subfamily, branches, subbranches, and languages. Dialects are regional variations of a language and might foretell future splitting.

Historical linguistics

Historical linguistics traces the origins, divergences, and movements of languages across space and time. However, to even begin to investigate historical linguistics, one must first understand the structure and classification of the various languages. Once these relationships are understood, research into the history of the various languages and groups can begin. One can look at a group of related languages and their geographic locations to propose an earlier common language. Or, one can look at the geographic distribution of a language to see if it is related to other nearby languages to propose movement of the language, and (possibly) people.

For example, even if one did not know anything about English, the distribution of English across the planet would suggest considerable movement of the language (and probably people too!). It would be perfectly reasonable to suggest considerable migration or a large empire, or both. An analysis of the geographically contiguous languages at the various places where English is spoken (e.g., Australia, the United States, India, South Africa) would show that the nearby languages were completely unrelated and that those from northwestern Europe were related. This pattern would indicate that English originated in northwestern Europe. In addition, a comparison of word lists could provide some idea of how long ago languages split.

From such analyses, we can learn where people came from, when (and perhaps even how) they migrated, how those societies changed over time, and what impact they had on other societies. However, there are a few languages, such as Basque (spoken primarily in northern Spain), that defy classification and might reflect very ancient language families.

Further, an examination of word lists can indicate areas a group formerly occupied, what resources were used in the past, and changes in technology over time. For example, even a brief examination of English will reveal a large number of currently used words and phrases (some as metaphors) that are associated with horses and horse technology, formerly of primary importance to everyone. These include "hold your horses" (have patience), "rein him in" (restrain someone), and "long in the tooth" (indication of old age).

Sociolinguistics

"Sociolinguistics" examines how social categories (such as age, sex, gender, ethnicity, religion, class, race, and even geography) influence the use and significance of distinctive styles of speech. Children talk in a particular way. Males and females can have distinct vocabularies (engendered speech), and foul language may be acceptable and even expected in some settings. Most languages have such variations for specific social situations. In a few cases, entire languages, such as Klingon, were created for entertainment value.

In many cases, professions and some other groups use specific terms and phrases not commonly used in everyday speech. The purpose of such speech, called "lexicon" or jargon, is to rapidly communicate specialized information. Excellent examples of lexicon are the vocabulary used by physicians, attorneys, police, and the military. Other examples include the various sports and technical disciplines. The term lexicon is part of the lexicon of anthropology.

Other specialized languages can be used for security purposes, such as computer encrypted data used by companies, governments, and the military. An interesting example of the use of this type of language is the "code talkers" in both World Wars. In those conflicts, the US military used Native Americans in different units to openly communicate over the radio so that the messages did not require decoding and could be quickly understood. The Native American languages were so foreign to the enemy that they could not be understood or "decoded." The most famous of the code talkers are the Navajo in the Pacific theater during World War Two.

Some other linguistic elements

Another important linguistic element is "metaphor," the use of words or phrases to convey some other meaning. For example, one could use the phrase "what's your kryptonite?" to inquire about weakness, or "another Vietnam" to refer to a military quagmire of some sort. However, to be able to understand the meaning of a metaphor, one must have the requisite background cultural knowledge; that is, unless you already know what "kryptonite" or "Vietnam" was, you would have no idea of the actual meaning of the phrases.

In addition, each language has specific voice effects, called "paralanguage." These sounds accompany speech and contribute to communication, such as crying, laughing, signing, grunting, and moaning. Body motions used to convey messages are called "gestures."

Writing

Writing is a system of visible or tactile symbols used to represent units of language following formal rules (e.g., grammar). The earliest known writing system is Mesopotamian cuneiform, dating as early as 6,000 years ago. Egyptian hieroglyphics were first used some 5,500 years ago. The first writing was to record commercial transactions. Systems to record narrative information, such as stories, originated with the development of alphabets. An alphabet is a series of symbols representing the sounds of language arranged in a specific order.

There are a number of ways to record information and not all records, or even narratives, are written using methods Westerners would recognize. One of the best examples of this is the Inka quipu (Figure 5.1), a system of bifurcated strings and knots thought to have been used just to keep records of products. However, it is now beginning to be realized that the quipu is far more complex than originally thought. On further examination, the quipu is made up of strings of different materials (plant fibers and hairs of different animals) and of different colors. This diversity of the number of strings, how they are split, their composition, their color, and the placement and type of knots results in a fantastically complex system that is now believed to include narrative information. So far, it remains undeciphered.

Why is writing important? In addition to the information that can be obtained by reading the writing of a society, archaeologists focus on writing as an indication of the political and economic complexity of a society. The reasoning is that if a society has writing (in whatever form) they must have had a system too

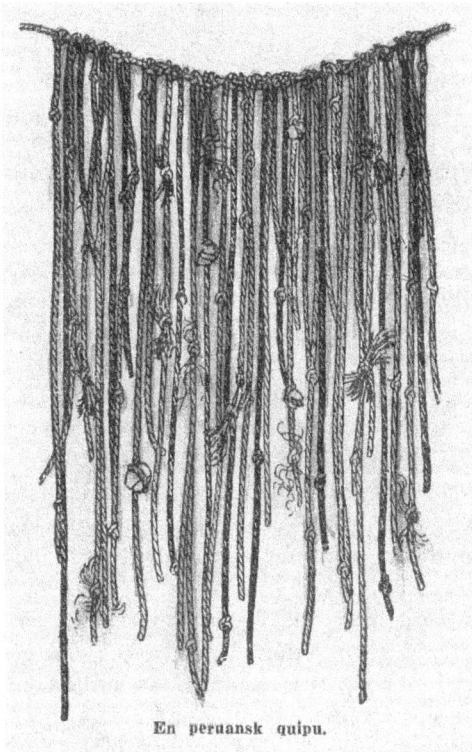

En peruansk quipu.

Figure 5.1 An Inka quipu (Alamy).

complex to function just based on peopling remembering things. Thus, writing is one of the criteria for the classification of a society as a state (see Chapter 7).

Chapter summary

Anthropological linguistics is the systematic study of all aspects of human language. Many of some 7,000 languages still spoken are in immediate danger of extinction. Following cognitive linguistics, the loss of a language also means the loss of a unique way of thinking and of human understanding. Anthropological linguistics can be divided into three major categories: descriptive, historical, and social.

Descriptive linguistics strives to understand the formal rules of a language. Grammar is the structure of a language, including the arrangement of clauses, phrases, and words in sentences and paragraphs. Morphology is the rules of word formation in a language, phonemes are distinct units of sound, while morphemes are the smallest units of sound that carry a meaning. Syntax is the set of rules regarding the assembly of phrases and sentences. Phonology is the study of the production, transmission, and reception of speech sounds. Languages are then classified in relation to other languages.

Historical linguistics traces the origins, divergences, and movements of languages across space and time. Related languages and their geographic locations can be traced back to an earlier common language and the movements of languages (and people) can be traced back in time. This can inform us about when and where people came from, how they changed over time, and what their past society was like.

Sociolinguistics examines the language variations used by different social groups, such as those based on age, sex, gender, ethnicity, religion, or class. It is common for professions and some other groups to use specific terms and phrases not commonly used in everyday speech. The purpose of such speech, called lexicon or jargon, is to rapidly communicate specialized information.

There are a number of other important linguistic elements. These include metaphor, the use of words or phrases to convey some other meaning, paralanguage, specific voice effects, and gestures, body motions used to convey messages.

Writing is a system of visible or tactile symbols used to represent units of language following formal rules (e.g., grammar). An alphabet is a series of symbols representing the sounds of language arranged in a specific order. Writing is an important source of information about a society and its presence suggests that the society in question had a complex economic and political system.

6 Social organization

Social organization is how a society is organized into groups of various kinds. Major aspects of social organization include kinship, marriage, nonkin organizations, inequality, and status and rank. Another major element of social organization is the political system, but this is generally considered separately (as it is here; see Chapter 7). Religion (see Chapter 10) may also be a factor in social organization. While all societies, large and small, have social organizations, each of them deals with these matters differently, making for remarkable variation across the world.

Kinship

A kinship system is used to determine who one's relatives are and to classify them for various reasons. This is critical since one has to know who is who, whom you can and cannot marry, what your status is, your inheritance, who you can ask for help, whom you are obligated to, and the like. Kinship also carries with it expectations of behavior. For example, one would treat their father quite differently than a stranger. A kinship organization tracks and classifies relatives based on descent through a series of parent-child links. Descent groups are a way each society can organize its members along kinship lines.

Families and households

A "family" is, broadly speaking, a group of relatives related by blood, marriage, or adoption. More specifically, families are commonly defined as groups of relatives living together in a single household. A "nuclear family" consists of the immediate family: the parents and children, but which may include a step-parent, stepsiblings, and adopted children. An "extended family" is generally seen as a larger set of relatives, such as grandparents, aunts and uncles, parent, and children, all living together. Another type is the blended family, several fragmented families reforming into a single family due to divorce and remarriage.

The "household" is the primary residential unit of a family, the home in which they live. It is also the center of economic production, consumption, child rearing, and shelter.

Figuring relatives

Everyone has relatives. In order to determine them, there must be a starting point and this reference person is called "Ego." People related to Ego by marriage, Ego's spouse or in-laws are called "affinal" relatives. People related by blood, such as Ego's parents and children, are called "consanguineal" relatives. Consanguineal relatives that are in a direct line to Ego, grandparents, parents, children, are called "lineal" while those not in a direct line, such as aunts and uncles, are called "collateral."

Cousins, in general, are the children of the siblings of Ego's parents, Ego's aunts and uncles. Cousins are recognized in Western societies but only in a general sense. However, in most societies, cousins are quite important and are classified into one of two types. "Cross-cousins" are the children of opposite sex sibling of parent, that is, mother's brother's children or father's sister's children. The children of the same sex sibling of the parent, father's brother or, mother's, sister, are called "parallel cousins." These cousin types are not important in the United States but figure prominently in several other major kinship systems.

Each person can be classified with a descriptive term and each has a kinship term, the specifics of which would depend on the system being used. For example, the descriptive term for father's brother is father's brother but in the United States, that person would be called uncle. A standard kinship diagram with descriptive terms is shown in Figure 6.1.

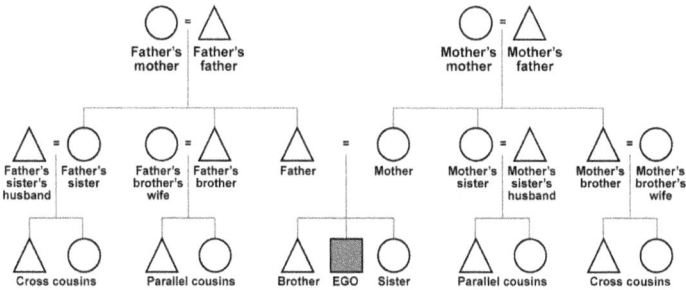

Figure 6.1 A standard kinship diagram with descriptive terms indicated (Ego is the reference point).

Sometime groups apply kinship terms to those that are not actually related, called "fictive kin." These may be people who are considered "family" for some reason, such as Godparents, or a Catholic Priest (called "Father"), or unrelated member of a social group (e.g., "sisters" in a sorority). In some cases, fictive kinship terms may be applied to animals out of respect, such as those that are hunted, sometimes called mother, father, sister, or brother.

Figuring descent

Each person belongs to a descent group, a "lineage," a group of lineal relatives from which one either descended (e.g., grandparents and parents) or has descendants (e.g., children). However, some societies do not include lineages within their kinship system. Lineal descent groups can be figured in one of several basic ways (there are other, uncommon, ways). First, one could figure descent through only one side of the lineal family, called "unilineal descent." If figured through the father's side ("patrilineal descent"), the descent group would include father and grandfather, but not mother or grandmother. If figured through the mother's side ("matrilineal descent"), the descent group would include mother and grandmother, but not father or grandfather. The children (both male and female) would

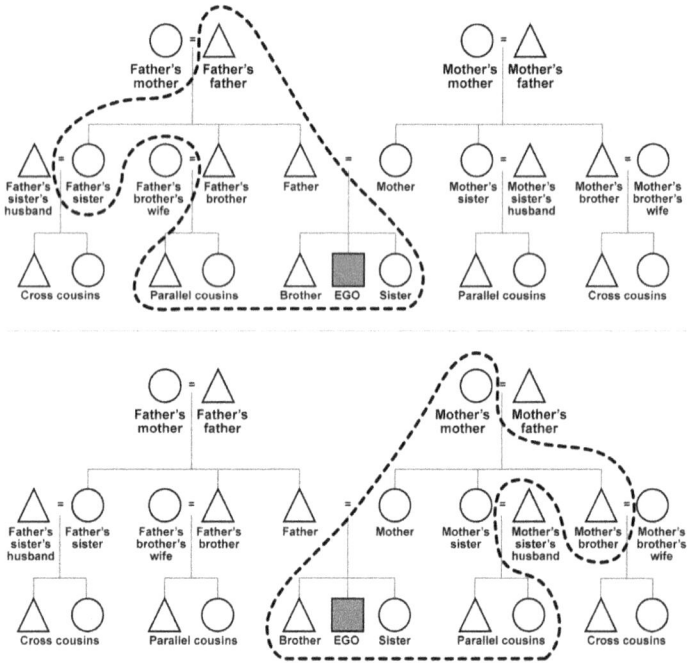

Figure 6.2 Patrilineal (top) and matrilineal (bottom) descent groups (circled) on a simple kinship diagram.

belong to the lineage of the designated parent, the mother in a matrilineage or the father in a patrilineage (Figure 6.2).

The other major approach is "bilateral descent," where the descent group is figured through both the mother's and father's sides at the same time, with (theoretically) no bias toward either side. The system used in the United States is bilateral, although there is a slight bias toward being patrilineal, seen, for example, in a wife taking the husband's last name. This a custom but not a rule.

Descent groups

There are a variety of descent groups configured in levels (Figure 6.3), with each being built on the previous level. Not

Organizational level (left to right)				
Family A		A family organization		
Family B				
Family A	Lineage A	A lineage organization		
Family B				
Family C	Lineage B			
Family D				
Family A	Lineage A	Clan A	A clan organization	
Family B				
Family C	Lineage B			
Family D				
Family E	Lineage C	Clan B		
Family F				
Family G	Lineage D			
Family H				
Family A	Lineage A	Clan A	Moiety A	A moiety organization
Family B				
Family C	Lineage B			
Family D				
Family E	Lineage C	Clan B		
Family F				
Family G	Lineage D			
Family H				
Family I	Lineage E	Clan C	Moiety B	
Family J				
Family K	Lineage F			
Family L				
Family M	Lineage G	Clan D		
Family N				
Family O	Lineage H			
Family P				

Figure 6.3 An illustration of descent group levels and complexity.

all kinship systems use all of the levels, but many do. The first level is that of the family, nuclear or extended and some systems do not extend beyond the family. This is true in the United States, making it one of the least complex kinship systems in the world.

The next level of complexity is that of the lineage, a unilineal kinship group that is descended from a common ancestor or founder where relationships among members can be traced genealogically from a real person over many generations. If a society has lineages, they might be organized into groups of lineages called "clans." Clans claim common descent from a remote ancestor, usually legendary or cosmological, such as Bear or Eagle. One cannot change their lineage or clan. Groups of people related to a living individual, even if not in one's lineage, are known as kindreds.

If a society has clans, those clans might be organized into groups. If clans are organized into two (and only two) groups, each such group is called a "moiety." The clans in a moiety would share some common element, such as Bear and Deer clans being members of a Mammal moiety and Eagle and Crow clans being members of a Bird moiety. Moiety membership cannot be changed. Moieties can have extremely important functions, such as in marriage, ranks, and being responsible for certain ceremonial cycles that guarantee the survival of the society.

If clans are organized into more than two groups of clans, each is called a "phratry." Membership in a phratry is flexible and clans can change their phratry membership if they wish. That said, phratry organizations are not very common.

Why are these organizations important? Membership in these organizations carries with it aspects of group and personal identity, rules about marriage, political structure, and responsibilities regarding ceremonial cycles and other societal functions. Westerners do not have such complex kinship organizations and so find it difficult to understand them. Perhaps an analogy would be subcultures (or political parties) in the Western societies.

Clans, moieties, and phratries claim ancient ancestors, often from cosmology, and it is common for them to adopt those ancestors as a "totem." A totem is a spirit animal or other entity embraced as a guardian. For example, if the claimed ancestor of a clan was Bear, the clan may be named the Bear clan and Bear might be its totem. A totem may be adopted by any number of other organizations (think the "totems" of American Sports teams, Bears, Rams, Dolphins, Padres, and the like). Individuals may also have totems, guardian spirits obtained during a puberty ceremony. Totemism is found in many areas of the world.

The major kinship systems

There are seven major kinship systems (there are other uncommon ones too), each with variation from society to society. A very basic description of each is provided below. Recall that L. H. Morgan (see Chapter 2) described most of the kinship systems and named them after Native American groups. Each person occupies a particular position that anthropologists can easily describe, such as mother's brother. However, each system will assign that person a particular label, such as Uncle, or Father (as shown in Table 6.1).

The "Hawaiian" system is bilateral, with a classification based on generations and is used in Hawai'i. In this system, everyone in your parent's generation is called mother and father and everyone in your generation is called brother and sister. Of course, everyone knows who their actual biological parents are and which "sisters" and "brothers" are not actually related and so eligible to marry. This system was quite confusing to the Christian missionaries who thought the Hawai'ians were literally marrying their siblings and this misunderstanding contributed to their poor treatment by Europeans. This system is still used today among native Hawai'ians.

The "Eskimo" system is bilateral and has an emphasis on nuclear family and includes the suffix of "in-law" to refer to affinal relatives. This system is used by the Inuit and is the same system used by most people in the United States.

The "Iroquois" system is unilinear, is generally matrilineal, and was named after the Iroquois that were intensively studied by Morgan. In this system, the same sex siblings of the parent are called by the same term as the parent and their children (parallel

Table 6.1 Terms applied to relatives[a] in the major kinship systems

System	General type	Relative's designations and what are called by system							
		Father's brother	Father's sister	Mothers' brother	Mother's sister	Paternal cross-cousins	Paternal parallel cousins	Maternal cross-cousins	Maternal parallel cousins
Hawai'ian	Bilateral, generational	Father	Mother	Father	Mother	Sister and brother	Sister and brother	Sister and brother	Sister and brother
Eskimo[b]	Bilateral	Uncle	Aunt	Uncle	Aunt	Cousins	Cousins	Cousins	Cousins
Iroquois	Unilinear	Father	"Aunt"	"Uncle"	Mother	Sister and brother	Cousins	Cousins	Sister and brother
Omaha	Unilinear	Father	"Aunt"	"Uncle"	Mother	Cousins	Cousins	Mother and father	Cousins
Crow	Unilinear	Father	"Aunt"	"Uncle"	Mother	Mother and father	Cousins	Cousins	Cousins
Sudanese	Bilateral	Each person has a unique term							

Source: Table by author.
Notes:
a In all systems, parents are called mother and father and siblings are called sister and brother. Aunt and uncle designations are used in a generic sense.
b The Eskimo system is the one generally used in the United States.

cousins) are called by the same terms as siblings. That is, mother's sister is called mother and her children are called brother and sister.

The "Omaha" system is unilinear and is generally associated with patrilineal societies. Here, the same sex siblings of the parent are called by the same term as the parent, so mother's sister is called mother and father's brother is called father. Next, the maternal cross-cousins (mother's sister's children) are "elevated" to the parental generation and given the same terms. That is, mother's brother's daughter(s) is called mother and mother's brother's son(s) is called father.

The "Crow" system is very similar to the Omaha system. The major difference is that instead of the maternal cross-cousins being elevated, the paternal cross-cousins (father's sister's children) are "elevated" to the parental generation and given the same terms. That is, father's sister's daughter(s) is called mother and father's sister's son(s) is called father.

The "Sudanese" system is bilateral and both complex and simple. In this system, each person has a unique designation. Thus, it is simple but it would be hard to remember everyone!

The last of the kinship systems, and by far the most complex, is the "Indigenous Australian Section System." This is a very intricate and dynamic system based on moieties, geography, ritual responsibilities, and in some places, biological sex. Depending on the specific society (there are some 500 in Australia), relatives might be divided into two sections (groups), four if sex (male/female) is also used. Other societies will divide people into 4 sections based on geography, 8 if sex is also used. Still other societies will use 8 sections (called subsections), 16 if sex is also used. One's kinship obligations, ritual responsibilities, and potential marriage partners are regulated depending on one's section or subsection and the complex connections between them.

Marriage

"Marriage" is the formal union between two or more people that is sanctioned by the society and is a cultural universal. This union establishes rights and obligations between the people and their children (and perhaps in-laws) and creates a family. There is considerable variation in the rules and practices of marriage and of divorce. In many societies, marriages are arranged by the family for a variety of reasons while marriage due to romantic love is uncommon as it is a fairly recent phenomenon.

The functions of marriage

Marriage is important for a number of reasons. It creates a family unit and formalizes and codifies the relationship so it is known to all. The family unit is an economic entity and since most societies have a sexual division of labor, most marriages involve a male/female unit. Reproduction is another important reason for a male/female union: to provide legitimacy for children (for status, rank, and inheritance), to establish responsibility for and care of children, to create an educational unit to enculturate the next generation, to regulate sexual access between spouses, and to form or reinforce political ties. However, in some societies, some of these reasons do not apply and marriage rules can vary, such as gay marriage in Western societies. Recently, the Pope sanctioned civil unions.

Some general marriage rules

Each society has a set of rules that govern marriage and is based on the kinship ties defined by each society (this is one of the reasons kinship is so important). The rules dictate who is an eligible marriage partner, who is not, how many spouses you can have, if you can get divorced, and the like. "Proscriptive rules" govern whom you cannot marry, for example, all societies prohibit marriage between immediate family members (called "incest"), although there are some exceptions (think royalty). "Prescriptive rules" govern whom you must or should marry. For example, "exogamy" (very common) states that one must marry someone outside your group (such as your clan or moiety) while "endogamy" states you must marry someone within your group, such as a prohibition on marrying an "outsider."

Types of marriages

There is considerable variety in the details of marriages from society to society and most fall under two broad general types,

monogamy and polygamy, with the latter divided into polygyny and polyandry. There are also marriages arraigned by the
family, still a common custom in many societies. Another type
is patterned marriages, such as an agreed upon system of mate
exchange between villages.

Monogamy

"Monogamy" is the marriage type where each person has just
one spouse. Most marriages are monogamous, even in societies that permit polygamy, and it is the only form recognized in
North America and most of Europe. There is no associated rule
of the spouses being of the opposite sex. "Serial monogamy" is
the marriage form whereby an individual marries (or lives with)
a series of partners in succession. Serial monogamy is increasingly common among North Americans as individuals divorce
and remarry.

Polygamy

"Polygamy" is when one individual has multiple spouses at the
same time. Polygamy is permitted in about 80–85% of the world's
societies and is the most preferred form of marriage worldwide,
although most individuals in those societies have monogamous
marriages. There are two types of polygamy, polygyny and
polyandry.

"Polygyny" is a male having multiple wives and this is the
most common form of polygamy. Such a marriage is desired for
a number of reasons. It asserts the wealth and status of the male
to other members of the society, it increases the labor potential of
the household, it allows for a greater number of children (ultimately for labor), it increases the number of sexual partners for
the male, and can generally increase wealth. On the downside,
there can be much greater conflict from jealousy or disputes over
authority in the household, and supporting multiple partners and
many children is expensive.

"Polyandry" is where a female has more than one husband. This is very uncommon and fewer than a dozen societies are known to have practiced polyandry. This practice can

limit population growth, which in turn, can alleviate increased pressure on resources. Marriage of one woman to two (or more) brothers prevents land from being fractured among sons. Plus, where males do a majority of subsistence labor, it can provide more male labor for family.

Postmarital residence

Once married, a couple has to live somewhere. There is an assortment of rules, with a variety of variations and exceptions, and so it can get complicated. However, there are three primary postmarital forms: patrilocal, matrilocal, and neolocal.

"Patrilocal" postmarital residence is the pattern in which a married couple lives in the locality associated with the husband's family and the bride must move to husband's band, tribe, or community. This is common in societies where men are dominant in the role of subsistence patterns. In patrilocality, it is common for the family of the groom to compensate the family of the bride for her leaving, a practice called "bridewealth". If the couple gets divorced, the bridewealth must be returned.

"Matrilocal" postmarital residence is the pattern in which a married couple lives in the locality associated with the wife's family and the groom must move to bride's band, tribe, or community. This practice is common to horticultural societies. No compensation is given to the family of either spouse.

"Neolocal" is the pattern in which a married couple establishes a new household in a location apart from either the husband's or the wife's relatives. This is common in industrial and post-industrial societies where independence is favored.

Divorce

"Divorce" is the formal ending of a marriage. Like marriage, divorce in most societies is a matter of great concern to the spouse's families because it impacts not only the individuals dissolving the marital relationship, but also the household, children, in-laws, and other relatives. In some societies, divorce is as simple as declaring it verbally and leaving the household. In some other societies, divorce can be very disruptive, especially if the family has wealth or major labor needs and cannot afford to lose a spouse. Some societies (and some religions) do not permit divorce, but it often happens anyway (recall ideal versus actual behavior).

Divorce rates are climbing around the world, but at the fastest rate is in Industrial societies. One theory regarding this is that prior to AD 1800, many marriages did not last longer than 10–20 years since people died before they were married that long. Today with better health care and preventative medicine, people are living much longer, possibly leading to a higher rate of divorce.

Non-kinship-based social organizations

People organize themselves in a wide variety of other, non-kinship-based, ways. Groups may be based on sex, gender, age, profession, interest (e.g., subcultures), or necessity. Individuals of different sexes (e.g., men and women) often form separate groups and these can be easily seen in most societies. Groups based on gender or sexual orientation are also obvious, particularly in Western societies.

Other obvious groups are based on age. "Age grades" are organizations whose members pass through a number of categories as they age. These are cultural universals and membership in them is not really optional. Some age grades might be limited to a rather narrow age group, such as school grades whose members are expected to be of a certain age (e.g., a 40-year-old college freshman would be out of place). Or, they might be more broadly based, such as child, adult, and senior. Thus, a person might belong to several age grades at the same time (e.g., First Grader and child). Transitioning between age grades may entail ceremonies or rituals (see rites of passage in Chapter 10), such as a puberty ceremony marking the change from an adolescent to an adult.

Sodalities

A "sodality" is an organization based not on kinship but on some common interest, activity, or occupation and is a cultural universal. Membership in a sodality is not automatic and is generally voluntary. Examples of sodalities include professional associations, sororities and fraternities, sport teams, service clubs, and the military.

Each sodality has some sort of entrance requirement. For example, admittance to a sorority is limited to females, generally of college age. Admittance to a professional association may require proof of qualification, for example, one has to be a physician to belong to the Association of Physicians. Or one may have to be a young male to belong to the warrior society of a particular society. Once the "warrior" becomes too old, they are removed from that organization, but may enter another designed for former warriors. An example of this is the young "War Chiefs" and the older "Peace Chiefs" of some Native American societies.

A person might be a member of several sodalities, a member of a warrior society and of a particular lacrosse team, an example taken from Native American groups in the Southeastern United States. A college student might at the same time be a member of a fraternity, the football team, the Art Club, and the ROTC. Interestingly, some sodalities will employ the use of fictive kinship terms to refer to their members, such as "sister" in a sorority or "brother" in an Army combat unit.

Inequality

Inequality is present in all societies. Inequality reflects differential access to resources, power, wealth, and the like. Some societies have relatively little inequality while others have very substantial inequalities that create a number of difficult issues. Inequality can see seen in regards to age, sex, salary, privilege, status, responsibility, and political power. For example, inequality can be seen by age in all societies and children do not have equal access to anything.

Societies with relatively little inequality are called "egalitarian." In such societies, often small ones, inequality is generally informal and based on age, sex, and ability. Many such societies have divisions of labor based on age and sex meaning it is likely that there is differential access to resources and power . Ability is also an issue as a skilled hunter will probably have more access to meat than a poorly skilled hunter and a skilled politician will more likely be a leader with some power.

Prescribed and institutionalized inequality is present in many societies where social strata are formalized. In these "stratified societies," inequality is an element of the overall social structure and is manifest in a variety of ways, including class, caste, rank, and status. It is common to view stratification as vertical (generational) but it is also horizontal, such as by sex, age, or membership in a clan.

Some societies have an institutionalized "class system," a social structure that generally have three or more "strata" or levels, such as lower class, middle class, or upper class (as is used in the United States). A class system is generally based on economics, such as how much money, or how many cattle, or how many wives, one has. While a person is born into the class of their parents, a class system allows for some mobility so it is possible to change class through one's ability and achievement.

A "caste system" is different. Like class, one is born into a caste but there is no mobility and one (generally) remains in the caste for life. Caste systems are fairly common and castes are often associated with a profession. For example, India has a very complex caste system, generally associated with Hinduism. The Brahman caste (priests and teachers) is at the top while the "untouchables," laborers that do work considered polluting, such as fishing, cleaning, butchering, and scavenging, are at the bottom (Figure 6.4). There are many prohibitions between the castes, such as people of a lower caste not being permitted to enter the house of a higher caste person, no sharing of food, and other practices akin to apartheid. Castes tend to be endogamous.

Although there is no mobility within the Indian caste system, it is possible for Hindus to "leave" the system by converting to another religion, such as Islam or Buddhism. But unless one moved, the neighbors would still know "who you are." The caste system in India was formally outlawed in about 1985 but that has not stopped its practice. A caste system also exists in Mexico.

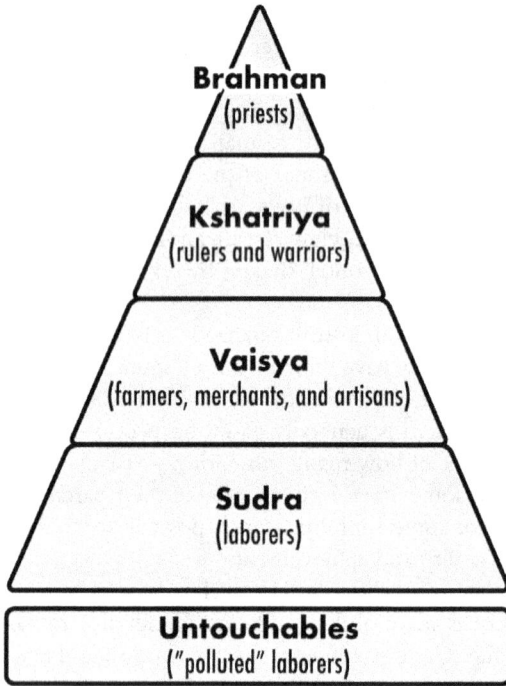

Figure 6.4 A simplified diagram of the caste system in India.

Status and rank

Each individual in every society has a "status," one's place in the society. Status tends to be informal, based on criteria such as age, sex, gender, education, wealth, ethics, or contributions. One's status can change, depending on what one does. "Rank" is a formalized status where people hold a specific position in a hierarchy with specific duties and responsibilities, such as in the military or political office. In some societies rank can be incredibly important. For example, among Native American groups in the Northwest Coast of North America, each person is ranked in a family, each family is ranked in its lineage, each lineage is ranked in its clan, each clan is ranked in its moiety, each moiety is ranked, and each village is ranked. It is a very complex system.

Both status and rank can be either achieved or ascribed. An "achieved" status or rank is one that is earned through talent and achievement, such as a competent soldier being promoted to a higher rank with greater responsibility. An "ascribed" status or rank is one that is given, not earned. An example of this is being born into royalty where you would automatically be a prince or princess without having to do anything.

Chapter summary

All societies have families, live in households, and have kinship and marriage systems, and each society deals with these matters differently. A kinship system is used to determine who one's relatives are so that one knows whom they can and cannot marry, their status, their inheritance, who they can ask for help, whom you are obligated to, and how to treat people.

A family is a group of relatives, living as either a nuclear family or an extended family. The household is the primary residential unit of a family, the home in which they live, and is the center of their economic activity, child rearing, and shelter.

Relatives that are related by marriage are classified as affinal and those related by blood are called consanguineal. Cousins are classified as either cross or parallel. Fictive kinship terms are sometimes applied to people that are unrelated and may also be applied animals out of respect, such as those that are hunted.

Descent is figured through lineal relatives. Lineal descent groups can be figured in one of several basic ways: either one side of the family (unilineal) or both sides (bilateral). If unilineal, descent may be figured through either the mother's side (matrilineal) or the father's side (patrilineal). In bilateral descent, the descent group is figured through both the mother's and father's sides at the same time.

Descent groups are configured in levels, with each being built on the previous one. The first level is that of the family, the second is the lineage, the third is the clan, and the fourth is the moiety (and phratry). Moiety membership cannot be changed but phratry membership is flexible. These organizations carry with them group and personal identity, rules about marriage, political structure, and responsibilities regarding ceremonial cycles and other societal functions.

There are seven major kinship systems. The Hawaiian system is bilateral and based on generations. The Eskimo system is bilateral and has an emphasis on nuclear family. The Iroquois system is unilinear and is generally matrilineal. The Omaha system is unilinear and is generally associated with patrilineal societies. The Crow system is very similar to the Omaha system. The Sudanese system is bilateral in which each person has a unique designation. Finally, the Indigenous Australian Section System, is very complex, with relatives being figured based on kinship sections, geography, and sometimes biological sex.

Marriage is the formal union between two or more people that establishes rights and obligations between the people and their children. Marriage creates a family unit, an economic unit, a reproductive unit, provides legitimacy for children and responsibility for their care and education, regulates sexual access, and forms or reinforces political ties. Proscriptive rules govern whom you cannot marry and prescriptive rules govern whom you must or should marry.

Most marriages fall under two broad general types, monogamy and polygamy, with the latter divided into polygyny and polyandry. Monogamy is the marriage type where each person has just one spouse. Serial monogamy is the marriage form whereby an individual marries (or lives with) a series of partners in succession. Polygamy is when one individual has multiple spouses at the same time. Within polygamy are polygyny, a male having multiple wives and polyandry, a female has more than one husband.

Once married, residence may be patrilocal, in which a married couple lives in the locality associated with the husband's family; matrilocal, the pattern in which a married couple lives in the locality associated with the wife's family; or neolocal, the pattern in which a married couple establishes a new household in a location apart from either the husband's or the wife's relatives.

Divorce is the formal ending of a marriage and can impact the spouses, the household, the children, the in-laws, and other relatives. In some societies, divorce is as simple, more challenging in others, and not permitted in some.

People organize themselves in a wide variety of ways that are based on non-kinship criteria such as sex, gender, or age. Sodalities are based on some common interest, activity, or occupation, such as professional associations, sororities and fraternities, sport teams, service clubs, and the military. A person might be a member of several sodalities.

Inequality, differential access to resources, is present in all societies. Societies with relatively little inequality are called egalitarian. Stratified societies have prescribed and institutionalized inequality and may include a class or caste system. A class system is commonly based on economics and it is possible to change class through one's ability and achievement. A caste system is different in that one is born into a caste and there is no way to change castes. Caste systems are fairly common and castes are often associated with a profession.

Each individual has a status, one's place in the society. Status tends to be informal and can change. Rank is a formalized status where people hold a specific position in a hierarchy with specific duties and responsibilities. Both status and rank can be either earned by one's actions and abilities achieved or ascribed. An achieved status or rank is one that is achieved through talent and action or ascribed (given) based on some criteria, such as royalty.

7 Political organization

Politics

"Politics" is, simply put, the process of decision-making. This process can take place between two people or two "polities" (e.g., formal organized political units). Each society has a political organization to both govern its own society and for its relations with other societies. Political organization is the way that power and authority is allocated, distributed, and embedded in society—the means by which a society creates and maintains social order, and to determine who gets what, when, and how.

Power and authority

"Power" is the ability to force some entity (person or society) do what you want. "Authority" is having the backing of the society to exert power. One can exert power without authority, such as an armed man robbing a store, who has the power (a gun) to force them to give him money, but has no authority to do so. The police that confront him in the parking lot of the store have both the power (guns) and the authority (being sworn officers) to stop him.

There are several methods used to wield power and to get a person or society to do what you want. The first is "persuasion," the use of negotiation and/or compromise (diplomacy) to exercise power. This is a very common method used by all people and societies. Diplomacy is commonly referred to as "soft power."

A second method is "coercion," the use of force or "hard power." Various levels of force can be used to maintain and ensure social control. A very minor example might be your professor "forcing" you to do a term paper for the class under the threat of a bad grade. An extreme form may be the society, backed by authority and through some enforcement entity, killing one of its members for some reason.

Lastly, the society can decide to exert military force against another society, through warfare. As has been noted by many, warfare is just another form of politics. Although this is a cynical view, it is also true.

Warfare

Warfare is the authorized and sanctioned use of military force: organized conflict between societies, or sometimes between "societies" such as criminal gangs. There is no rule about the scale or intensity of the conflict, only that be authorized. For example, if an individual decided on their own to get a gun and "invade" Canada, that would be a criminal act. If the United States government ordered that action, it would be warfare, what is commonly called "an act of war."

Warfare often involves the use of physical force, generally with weapons that can kill the enemy, and this is the most recognizable form. However, warfare can also be waged supernaturally, with the use of spirits and magic. For example, the Inuit and Cree in eastern Canada were at war for centuries but as both societies were very small, they rarely encountered each other to physically fight. Instead, war was waged by shamans who sought to kill the enemy using magic. The death of Inuit and Cree people was viewed as proof the magic worked.

Warfare can be very small scale, such as with the Inuit/Cree example above. Larger-scale warfare may be waged by larger groups, such as the Yanomamo of Venezuela and Brazil attacking other villages with war parties of dozens of men. The Dani in New Guinea are in a constant state of war, with a defended border, raids, and pitched battles with many hundreds of warriors. However, casualties are low and revenge for the last killing is a motivating factor. On the other end of the spectrum is "modern" warfare with millions of soldiers, huge numbers of casualties, and severe economic costs (not to mention nuclear war).

In addition to its varying scales and methods, warfare is conducted for a variety of reasons. These include to gain revenge, to gain territory, to obtain resources, to suppress or eliminate a people or a religion, or to gain strategic objectives.

It has also been argued that warfare is a recent phenomenon, tied to the rise of complex societies. Relatedly, some believe that hunter-gatherers do not have war because they generally lack complex political organizations, have small populations, rarely need outside resources, and have few possessions. But is this true? No, not as a blanket statement. Many hunter-gatherers do have complex political organizations and do engage in warfare. Even some small, less politically complex, hunter-gatherer societies are known to engage in warfare (recall the Inuit and the Cree).

Some anthropologists argue that warfare is a reflection of the innate aggressive nature of the human male. Others suggest warfare is "situation specific" and not an unavoidable expression of biological aggression. This is an important question, for if warfare is learned behavior rather than instinctive, perhaps we can learn not to engage in it. The presence of some nonviolent societies, such as the Semai and Amish, show support of the latter position.

The ideology of warfare

Warfare is usually accompanied by political, religious, or moral justifications that are embedded in a society's worldview. Everyone claims that "God" is on their side. Societies typically dehumanize the enemy so as to be able to justify the slaughter of men, women, and children. Carried to an extreme, it could result in genocide, the physical extermination of a society or ethnic group by another, either as a deliberate act or as the accidental outcome of activities carried out by one people with little regard for their impact on others.

Levels of political complexity

Every society has some form of political organization, some mechanism to regulate their members and for relations with other societies. The term "tribe" is commonly used by many people as a generic label for Fourth World groups. However, to anthropologists, the term tribe denotes a certain category of political complexity and has meaning in regard to population, leadership, and organization. Anthropologists generally recognize four categories of political complexity: band, tribe, chiefdom, and state, going from least complex to most complex (e.g., Service 1962). These terms only describe broad levels of political complexity and do not convey a judgment that one is better or worse than another.

Political complexity forms a continuum from rather simple to extraordinarily complex, with each society falling somewhere along the scale. Criteria for assignment to a particular level are rather vague so the assignment of a political system into one level rather than another should not be seen as definitive. A general framework of political complexity is shown in Table 7.1.

These levels of complexity do not represent a unilinear evolutionary scheme. It is simply a classification since all levels continue to exist today. However, it is generally true that as the population of a society increases, its political complexity also increases. It is also true that economic complexity is linked to increases in population and so increases in political complexity.

In many cases, irrespective of a society's actual political organization, European colonists and governments imposed (and still do) their own concept of hierarchical political authority on many of the traditional societies they encountered. The Europeans wanted to deal with a figure of authority, the "chief" of the "tribe." If such an individual could not be located (some societies did not have a "chief"), the Europeans would just pick a person, regardless of whether that person had any authority to speak for the society, and negotiations and/or ultimatums were made. If the society then failed to live up to the bargain made with that person, the society had "broken" the agreement and the door was open to retribution. The Europeans conveniently failed, or

Table 7.1 Major attributes[a] of the four primary levels of political complexity

Attribute/political level	Band	Tribe	Chiefdom	State
Population	Up to several hundred	Up to several thousand	Many thousands	More than many thousands
Mobility	Mobile	Sometimes mobile	Generally not mobile	Not mobile
Primary subsistence system	Hunting and gathering	Either hunter-gatherers or horticulturalists	Usually intensive agriculturalists but a few hunter-gatherers	Intensive agriculturalists
Ethnic identities	One	One	Usually one	May have several to many
Social structure	Family	Descent groups	Stratified	Highly stratified
Leadership	Egalitarian	Often egalitarian	Formal	Centralized
Exercise of power	Persuasion	Mostly persuasion	Persuasion and coercion	Mostly coercion
Specialization	No	No	Perhaps	Yes
e.g., Bureaucracy	No	No	Perhaps	Yes
e.g., Formal military	No	No	Perhaps	Yes
e.g., Public architecture	No	No	Sometimes	Yes

Source: Table by author.

Note:

a Remember that there are always exceptions to any rule.

even refused, to understand that most individuals they designated had no actual authority over their society, and that agreements made by that individual were not valid for the society as a whole.

Bands

The "band" is the least complex form of political organization. Bands are small, mobile, and egalitarian societies. Populations are typically small, numbering at most a few hundred people. All of the known bands are hunters and gatherers. Bands as a whole, called regional bands, may split-up periodically into smaller extended family groups (local bands) that are politically independent but will later reform back into their regional bands. Such a pattern is called "fission-fusion" and is commonly seasonal (e.g., apart in the winter, together in the summer).

A band may have a "leader," called a headman and typically male, but that person only has the power to persuade. Any actual decisions are made with the participation of the adult members, with an emphasis on achieving consensus but with the opinion of the headman serving as guidance. Headmanship is generally conferred on the most able person, but in some cases, the physically strongest male is the headman. Those unable to get along with the others of their band would move to another band where kinship ties give them rights of entry

Tribes

A "tribe" has a larger population than a band, may have several thousand members, and is more complex politically. People in a tribe are integrated by some unifying factor and share a common ancestry, identity, culture, language, and territory. Many tribes are hunter-gatherers but many others are horticultural and may be less mobile than some bands, although some, such as pastoralists, may be more mobile.

Tribes have formal leaders (office holders), typically males, who are called "chiefs" (by anthropologists). A tribe may have multiple offices, such as a council of chiefs or elders. Holders of these offices may be accomplished warriors or wise elders but, in some cases, political authority may lie with the clan, with clan elders regulating affairs. Although chiefs are formal leaders, they still have relatively little power but do have more authority and are thus better able to persuade people.

In some cases, polities that identify as tribes can be very large, even with millions of members. This is the case in many parts of the Middle East, Afghanistan, and Pakistan where tribal leaders are as important, or even more important, than the central government. It is important to understand this in any dealing with such countries with large tribes.

Chiefdoms

A "chiefdom" is a stratified polity in which two or more local groups are organized under a single leader, called a "chief" (not to be confused with a tribal chief), typically a male although some have very powerful females. Chiefdoms have multiple levels of a class or caste social system with the upper stratum being the privileged elite. Chiefdoms generally have relatively large populations, in the many thousands, with permanent (sedentary) settlements in several places under the central authority of the chiefdom. Anthropologists generally distinguish between "simple" chiefdoms and "complex" chiefdoms, the latter being a confederation of simple chiefdoms with a more complex hierarchy.

The "chief" occupies the top of the hierarchy. The office of the chief is usually for life, is often hereditary, and it is common for the chief to have real power. In many cases, offices of subchiefs exist and those people rule areas outside the central town. The considerable power and authority of the chief serves to unite his people in all affairs and at all times. Some of this power emanates from the control of esoteric knowledge, of ceremonies, and displays of wealth. The chief also usually controls the economic activities of the society and he may control a large amount of material wealth that can be used to show and maintain his status.

In some cases, chiefs or other men will strive to gain or maintain power and authority through the distribution, or redistribution, of food and prestige items. In many cases, these items may be obtained through favors or by "borrowing" materials to be paid back later. Once assembled, the individual holds an event to distribute the goods to members of the society. This results in the individual gaining considerable prestige and is thus considered a "Big Man" with influence in the society. This is analogous to borrowing money to throw a big party for important people.

Chiefdoms generally have large agricultural economies, although some are pastoralists. A few chiefdoms are of large and complex groups of hunter-gatherers, such as many of the societies along the Northwest Coast of North America.

States

A "state" is the most complex of the political organizations. States (here referring to early or preindustrial states) have large populations, numbering perhaps in the millions, many living in cities. Social organization is highly stratified into classes or castes organized and directed by a formal centralized government. Nearly all of the early states so far known were based on intensive agriculture, although one, the Mongols, was based on pastoralism. The earliest state-level societies appeared about 5,000 years ago and some states later developed into empires.

There are a number of criteria used to define a state, each of which is intended to demonstrate the power and authority of the central government. These include the power and authority to use force to defend the social order, the presence of a bureaucracy, codified law, writing (see Chapter 5), monumental architecture (e.g., pyramids), and a military to defend defined borders.

Until recently, early states were called "Civilizations" and this term remains commonly used. But Civilization is a poor choice of terms since the implication is that if a society was not a Civilization, its members are not civilized. This, of course, is wildly untrue. Now, the term state, or early state, is preferred.

Chapter summary

Politics is the process of decision-making, to exert control. Each society has a political organization to both govern its own society and for relations with other societies. Power is the ability to force some entity (person or society) to do what you want. Authority is having the backing of the society to exert power. There are several methods used to wield power, including persuasion (negotiation and/or compromise) and coercion, the use of force, including military force or warfare.

Warfare is the authorized and sanctioned use of military force, either using physical force or supernatural force. Warfare can range from very small scale, with few casualties, to world-wide with tens of millions of dead. Warfare is conducted for a variety of reasons, including to gain revenge, to gain territory, to obtain resources, to suppress or eliminate a people or a religion, or to gain strategic objectives. It is not clear whether warfare is a reflection of the innate aggression or learned behavior, if the latter, perhaps we can learn not to engage in warfare. Warfare is usually accompanied by political, religious, or moral rationalizations and societies typically dehumanize the enemy so as to be able to justify their slaughter.

Every society has some form of political organization to regulate their members and for relations with other societies. Anthropologists generally recognize four categories of political complexity: band, tribe, chiefdom, and state, going from least complex to most complex. These terms only describe broad levels of political complexity; they do not convey a judgment that one is better or worse than another. Nor do they represent a unilinear evolutionary scheme.

The band is the least complex form of political organization. Bands are small, mobile, and egalitarian hunter-gatherer societies. The leader of a band is called a headman but that person only has the power to persuade. Any actual decisions are made with the participation of the adult members, with an emphasis on achieving consensus.

A tribe has a larger population, up to several thousand (although a few are much larger). Many tribes are hunter-gatherers but many others are horticultural. Tribes have formal leaders (office holders), typically males, who are called "chiefs." Although chiefs are formal leaders, they still have relatively little power but do have more authority and are thus better able to persuade people.

A chiefdom is a stratified polity in which two or more local groups are organized under a single leader, called a "chief." Chiefdoms generally have relatively large populations, in the many thousands, with permanent settlements in several places under the central authority of the chiefdom. Social stratification is typical, either a class or caste with the upper stratum being the privileged elite. The office of the chief is usually for life and is often hereditary. It is common for the chief to have real power. The considerable power and authority of the chief serves to unite his people in all affairs and at all times. Chiefdoms generally have large agricultural economies, although some are pastoralists.

A state is the most complex of the political organizations. States (ancient or preindustrial states) have large populations living in cities with a highly stratified social organization and a centralized government. All of the early states so far known are based on intensive agriculture. States also have a bureaucracy, codified law, writing, monumental architecture (e.g., pyramids), and a military to defend defined borders. Formerly called "Civilizations," these polities are now called early states.

8 Economic organization

Everybody has to make a living and thus, each society has an economic system. Such systems can be hunting and gathering wild foods, doing small-scale farming, focusing on domesticated animals, or going all in as large-scale farmers. None of these types are exclusive and most economies are mixed.

An economic system can be divided into three basic components: production, exchange, and consumption. "Production" is making things: food, goods, and services. Once produced, there has to be a way, an "exchange" system, to distribute what was produced. "Consumption" is using things, thus creating a need to produce and exchange more items and is the simplest part of the system.

Production

Production requires labor, organization, and technology. For example, if you eat deer as a part of your diet, how do you get deer? Someone has to go hunting and someone has to butcher and cook the deer (labor), there has to be a system to support the hunter and the other people involved in the processing (organization), and the hunter has to have weapons to kill the deer and tools to process it (technology). Even what seems to be a simple deer hunt can be a complex endeavor and this process applies to all production.

Division of labor

All societies have a division of labor, most commonly divided by sex and age but also perhaps by gender, education, status, and even ethnicity. Division of labor organizes responsibilities for aspects of production. For example, in small societies where wild resources form the basis of the economy, males do the hunting while females gather wild plant foods. This division is present not because females are not inherently capable, but since they are commonly taking care of children (e.g., nursing), they are not mobile enough to chase game.

Divisions by age are also common. Children are unskilled and cannot be relied on to produce much. However, they can still contribute in a number of ways, such as helping to gather or carry materials. The elderly may no longer be capable of strenuous activities (e.g., hunting, gathering, heavy labor) but they can contribute as sources of knowledge and experience, in child care, and routine domestic tasks.

In Western societies, divisions of labor are also fairly common but are rapidly breaking down. For example, females now commonly occupy positions that had traditionally been occupied by males, such as firefighters, doctors, politicians, and combat soldiers. Societies evolve.

Exchange systems

Once something is produced, it has to be distributed throughout the economy. Most such distribution is accomplished by exchange—providing one thing for another. There are four basic systems of exchange and each can be used in combination with each other. The exchange systems are reciprocity, redistribution, barter, and market. But before anything can be exchanged, it has to have a value.

Value

Most things that are produced have two basic types of values: an economic value and a social value. Economic values can be immediate (e.g., food), diminishing (e.g., depreciation of a car), stable, or increasing (e.g., most real estate).

Social values may overlap with economic values. For example, everyone has to have food, but having caviar instead of a hamburger is beyond simple dietary needs and falls more into status. In some societies, it is necessary to have a canoe for fishing but some will have very fancy ones to impress people. One can see the same thing in Western societies, one may need a car for transportation but do you really need a Rolls Royce to get somewhere?

Finally, many things will have a ceremonial (or perhaps sentimental) value separate from other values. For example, an object associated with the creation of the world (following a particular cosmology) would have immense ceremonial or religious value but would have no economic value.

The reciprocity exchange system

"Reciprocity" is the exchange of goods and services between two parties in which one party give goods or services to someone with no expectation of an immediate return. There is, however, an expectation of eventual return. Generalized reciprocity is rather informal, where the precise value of the material not specifically calculated nor is the time of repayment specified. An example of this is a birthday gift or picking up a dinner check. Nothing is said at the time, but the giving party does expect the other party to eventually respond in kind. Balanced reciprocity is an exchange in which the giving and the receiving are specific as to the value of the goods or services at the time of their delivery.

The redistribution exchange system

"Redistribution" is the form of exchange in which goods flow into a central place where they are sorted, counted, and reallocated. This type of exchange system could work well in a small society where there were a relatively small number of people needing goods but if the group is too large, disparities in redistribution would quickly appear. To make it work, there must be some sort of control of the collected goods, perhaps by a chief or Big Man.

In larger societies with some sort of centralized government, goods in the form of gifts, tribute, taxes, and the spoils of war would be gathered into storehouses and redistributed from there. However, in large societies, any redistribution would have to be adjunct to another exchange system.

The barter exchange system

"Barter" is a system in which two or more parties negotiate a direct exchange of one thing (a good or service) for another, essentially a system of personal supply and demand. As each party seeks to get the best possible deal, both may negotiate until a balance has been reached where each party feels satisfied at having achieved the better of the deal. Although barter can involve just the direct exchange of a good or service, such as ten fish for one pig, it commonly involves the use of money. Barter is common in most societies, even in Western ones such as buying a car or a house that involves personal negotiation over price.

Money

What is "money"? The simple answer is that money is whatever you want it to be, as long as everyone agrees to recognize it. In many societies, money has some value from the effort it may take to manufacture it, perhaps from a material difficult to get or difficult to properly decorate. A wide range of things that have been used as money in one or another society includes salt, shells, stones, beads, feathers, fur, bones, teeth, metal, and paper (Figure 8.1).

Contemporary nation-states all have their own money, much of which is made from paper, a material with virtually no actual value. Its value derives from the agreement of everyone to use it. In some cases, paper money is backed by materials, such as gold, that have an actual value due to their use in industry. Today there are cryptocurrencies (e.g., Bitcoin) that are not even tangible.

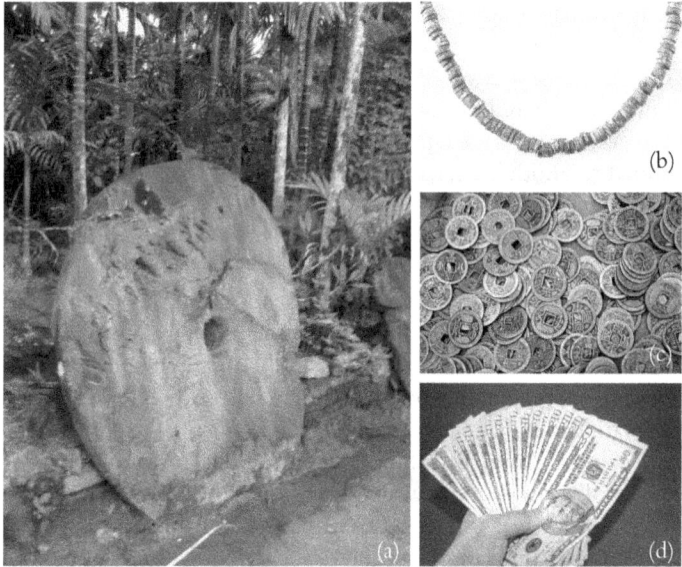

Figure 8.1 Money made from different materials: (a) Stone money from Yap, an island in the South Pacific (photo by David Weekly, Wikimedia Commons). (b) Ancient American Southwest shell bead money (Alamy). (c) Ancient Chinese metal money (Pixabay). (d) Contemporary Nation-state paper money (photo by Dani Simmonds, FreeImages).

The market exchange system

A "market" system in one in which the buying and selling of goods and services is done using money. Prices are set by rules of general supply and demand rather than any personal supply and demand as in barter. Money is used to make payments for goods and services as well as a way to measure value. Most market systems, such as in the United States, will include aspects of the three other systems, especially barter.

But a market system can be bifurcated. On Palau in the South Pacific, men and women had separate money systems used for different purposes. Women's money (decorated turtle shells) was used for regular, everyday purchases, such as food or other goods. Men's money (fragments of old European glass) was used solely to buy and sell canoes, with the goal of eventually having the best canoe.

The "secret economy": the black market

In many economies, the exchange of various goods or services is done in "secret" so as to avoid law, regulation, taxation, monitoring, or auditing. Such transactions are generally paid in cash and is commonly referred to as the "black market." Examples of such illegal transactions include drugs, weapons, sex, alcohol, stolen goods, endangered animals or their parts (e.g., ivory), and human organs such as kidneys. Less disturbing examples include mundane work done "off the books," such as child care, house cleaning, and gardening.

Basic subsistence systems

Societies are commonly characterized by anthropologists (and others) by their basic subsistence strategy, generally the most visible or important aspect of how they make their living. A subsistence system can be seen as a means of production but it is important to remember that subsistence involves more than just what you eat, it is also dependent on organization and technology. Subsistence systems are generally divided into four basic categories: (1) hunting and gathering, (2) horticulture, (3) pastoralism, and (4) intensive agriculture (Table 8.1). The latter three rely on the use of domesticated plants and animals.

Domestication and the development of agriculture

Domestication is the process of by which something comes under control. This could apply to the universe, landscapes, a river, or people. But most people use a narrower definition, one related to domesticated species related to agriculture. In that context, a domesticated species is one that humans have developed some intentional and detectable genetic control, such

Table 8.1 A summary of the major subsistence systems

Type	Emphasis	Characteristics
Hunting and gathering	Use of wild plants and animals, may use some horticulture	Generally mobile, small-scale societies but sometimes large and sedentary societies
Horticulture	Primarily domesticated plants and small animals; hunting and gathering often remains important	Small-scale individual production, only human labor
Pastoralism	Domesticated large animals and some plants, some hunting and gathering	Small- to large-scale, generally mobile
Intensive agriculture	Domesticated plants and animals generally raised in large numbers, very minor use of hunting and gathering	Large-scale, use of labor supplements (animals or machines)

Source: Table by author.

that the domesticated form is different from anything in the wild. Agriculture is the use of domesticated species for food and materials.

There are a number of theories of the origin of agriculture (e.g., Barker 2009). All people everywhere had been hunter-gatherers for millions of years, but then at the end of the Pleistocene about 10,000 years ago, the general environment warmed and populations expanded, major factors in the initiation of the process of domestication and agriculture (Kavanagh et al. 2018). Why, then, did people abandon a relatively stable and productive hunting and gathering strategy to take up agriculture, an economic pursuit that requires more labor and is subject to catastrophic crop failure? No one knows for sure.

Whatever happened, once people began the process of domestication of wild plants and animals and then became dependent on them, populations increased and congregated with an increase in political complexity and specialization. Over time, states developed.

However, farming is not necessary such a great thing, even though we are now "addicted" to it. Agriculture impacts the natural populations of the species domesticated, results in gigantic modification of ecosystems for farming, and overtaxes water and soil. As human populations grow and crowd together, they become susceptible to famine from crop failures, to greater warfare, and to pandemics (most recently Covid-19) as a result of living close together in cities.

Hunting and gathering

Societies whose subsistence system is hunting and gathering make their primary living from obtaining wild foods. Until the advent of agriculture about 10,000 years ago, all people subsisted as "hunter-gatherers." Today, most people are farmers. Even though hunting is the first word in the label, in fact, most of the food obtained by hunter-gatherers comes from gathering plants (with a few exceptions). In some cases, hunter-gatherers also practice some small-scale farming (horticulture, see below) as a minor part of the subsistence system.

Hunter-gatherer societies have a vast range of structures, forms, and adaptations (Kelly 1995). Many have band- or tribe-level political organizations and have relatively small, mobile populations. In many cases, these relatively small groups are called **foragers**. Other hunter-gatherer groups are much larger with more complex social and political systems, including tribes and chiefdoms. Their religion, literature, art, and music is intricate and varied. Most hunter-gatherers are egalitarian, have a simple division of labor based on sex and age, and are generally viewed as peaceful (there are exceptions). Further, hunter-gatherers are generally seen as living in marginal environments, but 10,000 years ago, they were in all environments. In the intervening 10,000 years, farmers have pushed them out of the more productive environments into the marginal ones.

Anthropologists often see contemporary hunter-gatherers as "living fossils" and use them as analogs for studying ancient human societies. While this analogy can be useful, it must be remembered that contemporary hunter-gatherers are alive *today* and therefore cannot be identical to ancient societies.

Finally, it is important to realize that *all societies*, including Western ones, continue to include hunting and gathering in their overall subsistence systems, as illustrated by our continuing love affair with hunting and fishing. But there is also a practical issue: the retention of the knowledge of how to "live on wild foods" was most useful during the Great Depression of the 1930s and continues to be part of military training.

Horticulture

Horticulture is, essentially, low-intensity agriculture involving relatively small-scale fields, plots, and gardens (Sutton and Anderson 2014). Both domesticated plants and small animals (e.g., pigs and chickens) can be part of horticultural systems and labor is by hand. Food is raised primarily for personal consumption rather than being traded or given to a central authority. Horticultural systems generally support relatively small and/or dispersed populations (there are exceptions) and are broadly associated with tribe-level political systems. Horticulturalists continue to hunt and gather wild foods but not as their primary source of food.

A number of types of gardens are used by horticulturists. These include small, individual gardens, raised fields, chinampas (raised fields in marshes), and terraced fields, many of which can be highly productive. A common garden type is the slash-and-burn field (Figure 8.2), where the vegetation in a small area is cut down, left to dry, burned, with crops then planted in the ashy soil. Such fields can only be used for a few years due to poor soils and are then abandoned with a new one being made. This system is not generally organized and fields can be put most anywhere, but this requires a large amount of available land.

A swidden system is a sustainable horticultural method involving the use of slash-and-burn fields but with a planned rotation of those fields over many years. Fields would be slashed and burned, abandoned, monitored over time until the soil recovered, then reused in a planned pattern. This system requires less land but is more susceptible to error since if fields are used

Figure 8.2 A slash-and-burn field in a small village near Chi Phat, Cambodia (Alamy).

again before they have recovered, production will be less and that can cause problems.

Pastoralism

"Pastoralism" is a system that focuses on animal husbandry: the herding, breeding, consumption, and use of various (large) domesticated animals (Sutton and Anderson 2014). Plant cultivation generally is not part of this system but there might be some horticulture and some crops may be obtained in trade. Hunting and gathering remains a minor, but often still important, pursuit. Pastoralism can support relatively large populations with fairly complex political systems and most are tribes. However, there are a few chiefdom-level pastoralist societies and one, the Mongols, developed a state-level political system and established the largest land empire ever known.

Pastoralists, sometimes called "nomads," focus on a number of animals, including cattle, horses, sheep, camels, goats, yaks, llamas, and reindeer. In many cases, pastoralists will move their animals from pasture to pasture depending on the season, such as summer in one and winter in another and large tracks of land for pastures are often needed. A great deal of knowledge about the pastures and animals is required to be successful, such as knowing what animals go in what type of pasture (different animals eat different things), how many animals and how long to leave them, when to return, and where to move next.

The primary products obtained from the animals include food (meat, milk, and blood), products (bone, manure, and hair), and labor. While people exploit the animals, the animals also get something out of the arrangement, including being provided food, protection, and guaranteed reproduction and species survival, even though most individuals are usually killed. In the United States and other Western countries, pastoralism is integrated into the overall intensive agricultural system.

One of the more interesting pastoralist systems is called "milch pastoralism," in which animal products, such as milk, are used without killing the animal, and so ultimately getting more food value from each animal (Galvin et al. 1994). Blood is another major product that can be obtained without killing the animal. About a quart of blood can be taken from a cow of either sex about once a month without damaging its health. Hair and wool can also be taken from live animals and made into many products. Manure is also a major animal product and can be used as fuel, as plaster in construction, and as fertilizer for the pastures or traded to farmers for use in their fields.

Intensive agriculture

"Intensive agriculture" is a large-scale and complex system of farming and pastoralism usually involving the use of supplemental labor, irrigation, and the production of surpluses (Sutton and Anderson 2014). Intensive agriculture represents a significant shift in the scale and scope of agriculture and reflects a fundamental change in the relationship between people and the environment. Many intensive agricultural societies (e.g., the United States) have a worldview that places themselves above nature with the belief that nature must be controlled and/or conquered. However, this is a flawed, and potentially catastrophic, view since all societies are integrated with their environment and none can escape the consequences of their actions.

The use of domesticated animals to supplement human labor is significant, although there are a few intensive systems that rely solely on human labor. This extra labor, plus irrigation, allows farmers to colonize new lands (and displace hunter-gatherers). Intensive agricultural systems also focus on just a narrow range of domestic species (mostly grains), with increases in both productivity and risk (if a crop fails, famine may result). Components of the other subsistence systems—hunting and gathering, horticulture, and pastoralism—continue to be used.

A consequence of the increased productivity of intensive agriculture is a massive increase in population. This results in greater sociopolitical complexity, reduction of mobility, nucleation of settlements, and the eventual evolution of state-level societies. While this cause and effect relationship between agriculture, population increase, and the development of states is overly simplistic, the trend is generally true.

The system used in most Western societies, and now being adopted by many other groups, is industrialized agriculture. This system is highly dependent on the extensive use of machines, fossil fuels, chemical fertilizers, pesticides, and herbicides, all of which require a vast industrial complex for support. In addition, the system results in very extensive landscape modification, such as damming and diverting rivers, draining marshes and swamps, and leveling land, all to the detriment of natural ecosystems. Although this system is highly productive, it is also highly polluting and very expensive. In the long run, it cannot be sustained, particularly as populations continue to increase.

Chapter summary

Each society has an economic system, hunting and gathering wild foods, doing small-scale farming, focusing on domesticated animals, or being large-scale farmers, all of which may contain elements of the others. An economic system can be divided into three basic components: production, exchange, and consumption. Production is making things: food, goods, and services. Once produced, there has to be a way, an exchange system, to distribute what was produced. Consumption is using things, thus creating a need to produce and exchange more items and is the simplest part of the system.

All societies also have a division of labor, often divided by sex and age, which organizes responsibilities for aspects of production. Men generally do the heavy labor and hunting; women generally do the gathering and domestic work; and children and the elderly do support tasks.

Goods and services have to be distributed, or exchanged, throughout the economy. There are four basic systems of exchange: reciprocity, redistribution, barter, and market. The value of goods and services depends on a number of factors, such whether it is economic, social, or ceremonial.

"Reciprocity" is the exchange of goods and services between two parties with an expectation eventual return. "Redistribution" is the form of exchange in which goods flow into a central place where they are sorted, counted, and reallocated. "Barter" is a system in which two or more parties negotiate a direct exchange of goods or services, although money may be used. Money is defined by the society and may take any form agreed upon, such as paper, metal, shell, or stone. A "market" system is one in which the buying and selling of goods and services is impersonal and done using money. A portion of most economies is done in secret, outside the rules, and is called the black market.

In addition to other aspects of an economy, each society has a basic subsistence system, one that produces food and other goods but is also dependent on organization and technology. Anthropologists typically recognize four basic systems: (1) hunting and gathering, (2) horticulture, (3) pastoralism, and (4) intensive agriculture, of which the latter three rely on the use of domesticated plants and animals. Domestication is the process of by which something comes under control and domesticated species are those under genetic control.

Agriculture, the use of domesticated species, was developed about 10,000 years ago in half a dozen places around the world. It is not clear why this happened but over time, people became dependent on farming and as populations increased and congregated, political complexity also increased and early states eventually. However, farming has a down side, such as environmental degradation and people being more impacted by war, disease, and famine.

Hunter-gatherers rely on wild foods, a system used by all people until about 10,000 years ago. Most of the food obtained by hunter-gatherers comes from plants and most hunter-gatherer societies are small and mobile with band-level political organizations, although there are some notable exceptions. Some hunter-gatherers also have some horticulture. Contemporary hunter-gatherers are not "living fossils" but are alive today and cannot be identical to ancient societies. Hunting and gathering continues to be used by all societies.

Horticulture is, essentially, low-intensity agriculture involving relatively small-scale fields, plots, and gardens with labor being human and food raised for personal consumption. Most horticultural systems support relatively small and/or dispersed populations and are associated with tribe-level political systems. Horticulturalists continue to hunt and gather wild foods but not as their primary source of food.

Pastoralism is a system that focuses on the various domesticated animals but may include some horticulture and hunting and gathering. Pastoralism can support relatively large populations with fairly complex political systems and most are tribes. Pastoralists use a variety of animals, including cattle, horses, sheep, camels, goats, yaks, llamas, and reindeer and will move their animals from pasture to pasture. Animals products include food (meat, milk, and blood), products (bone, manure, and hair), and labor.

Intensive agriculture is a large-scale and system of farming and pastoralism usually involving the use of supplemental labor, irrigation, and the production of surpluses. This results in greater sociopolitical complexity, reduction of mobility, nucleation of settlements, and the eventual evolution of state-level societies. Domesticated animals are usually used to supplement human labor and this extra labor, plus irrigation, allows farmers to colonize new lands. Intensive agricultural systems also focus just on grains with increases in both productivity and risk. Hunting and gathering, horticulture, and pastoralism continue to be used. Industrialized agriculture requires a vast industrial complex for support, is very polluting, has major consequences for natural ecosystems, and in the long run, cannot be sustained.

9 Identity

The identity of a person has many layers, including being a member of a variety of different groups and holding different positions within those groups. A person is first a member of a society and generally has an identified place/status within that society. A person is also a member of a family and may have several accompanying family identities. One may also be identified as a member of a socially constructed race, ethnic group, and/ or subculture. Lastly, a person has a personal, perhaps private, identity comprised of many elements, including sex and gender.

Societal identity

People are automatically members of the society in which they were born and there is no choice involved. Each person is enculturated into that society and would adopt the same basic aspects of that society, language, religion, and worldview. Even if one were to move to a new society, they would still be members of their original society, although that could change over several generations.

Individuals would have an inter-societal identity associated with elements such as age (e.g., child or adult), sex (e.g., male or female), rank (e.g., leader or follower), status (e.g., rich or poor; married or single), profession (e.g., farmer or fisherman), and the like. Some of these identities will change over time.

Family identity

Each person is also born into a family, each of which will have its own identity, such as a status or rank. A major event in establishing a family (and personal) identity is being given a personal name. This event establishes a person as being a member of the family (and society) and formalizes their birthright and social identity. Naming ceremonies are special events or rituals that mark one's existence as a person. Some societies will give a name prior to birth (e.g., in the United States), while others will do it at birth.

Some societies will wait to give names, sometimes for a year or more. If the child is not named, it is not yet defined as a member of the family or society and so is not really human. Such practices are seen in groups with high infant mortality or difficult living conditions. If the group decides it cannot care for a new member, the infant may be killed (infanticide) to go "back in line" to be born at a better time (reincarnation). It is not considered murder since they are not yet humans and is just a delay. This is a reflection of the worldview on who is human.

Each member of a family will have varying identities within that family. A person may be mother, daughter, aunt, and cousin at the same time but to different people. Each of these familial identities carries with them certain behaviors and responsibilities.

Socially constructed identities

People can also be identified by others as being members of other groups within the larger society. In many small societies, such groups do not exist. In larger societies, there may be a variety of subgroups based on appearance, origin, or behavior. In some cases, identity may be announced by the use of visible symbols, such as clothing, decoration, or body modification (e.g., tattoos or scarification).

Race

Humans are virtually identical genetically and we are all members of the same subspecies of human (*Homo sapiens sapiens*). There is some variation, typically due to adaptations to environmental pressures. Some of this variation, such as blood type, tissue type, sensory ability, and other features, are not obvious or easily detectable. Other features are visible and include morphology (e.g., height and weight), hair color, eye color, and skin color. Since skin color is the most visible, it has been used to group people into "races."

But as the concept of race is nearly meaningless biologically, the classification of people into these groups is a social construction, generally based on some bias of the classifier against the classified. Unfortunately, these classifications can be culturally important for a number of reasons, such as oppression. One only need to look at the treatment of nonwhite minorities in the United States to realize the damage such a social construct can do (e.g., Delgado and Stefancic 2017).

Ethnic groups

In large societies, such as the United States, there are communities of people from other societies who collectively and publicly identify themselves as a distinct group based on various cultural features such as shared ancestry and common origin, language, customs, and traditional beliefs. These "ethnic groups" might continue to speak their original language, practice their original religion, and still eat their own foods (which provides the basis of the many ethnic restaurants we all enjoy). At the same time, the members of these distinctive ethnic groups will generally acculturate into, and be dependent upon, the parent society. Thus, an ethnic group will exclude some traits and individuals from their group while at the same time, include others (Barth 1969).

In the United States, ethnic groups include more than 700 Native American Fourth World groups, plus some 300 other groups originally from other countries, such as Vietnamese-Americans, Italian-Americans, Mexican-Americans, and many more, each contributing to the mosaic of our multiethnic society.

A person may wish to "self-identify" as a member of an ethnic group, such as Native American. Such "wantabees" can be an issue, such as, when a member of an "oppressor" group wants to become a member of an "oppressed" group. In the case of Native Americans, this is rarely recognized by the tribes due to strict membership rules.

Subcultures

"Subcultures" are relatively small groups with distinctive variations of, and within, the primary society. A subculture may have their own standards and behavior patterns while still sharing common standards with the larger society. For example, members of a motorcycle club will have distinctive behavior, dress, and outlook but these traits will still be within the range of acceptable behaviors within the society (if that behavior crossed into being unacceptable, there would be repercussions). Other examples would include members of the New Age movement, surfers, cowboys, the military, professional athletes, and many more.

Some subcultures may develop to the point of being a separate society of sorts. Some street gangs have many of the elements of an independent society and behaviors outside of the accepted norms (e.g., being illegal) of the primary society. Some drug cartels might also be considered separate societies. They may have their own administrative organizations, health systems, education systems, and the like. However, whatever their anthropological classification, they are still considered criminal organizations by most nation-states.

Personal identity

In addition to one's societal and family identity, a personal identity must also be established. This is largely under the control of the individual, who exercises "agency," the ability to make their own choices. One's sex is not an initial personal decision but it might be changed in adulthood. Gender is usually expressed after childhood and then has to be has to be expressed (or hidden). Westerners tend to conflate sex and gender, making it difficult for them to understand the different identities that may result.

Sex

Sex is a biological classification based on external (visible) reproductive anatomy, either a penis or a vagina. This forms a binary classification: either male or female. The assignment of sex is quite important in societies that have a distinct "division of labor" based on sex, such as in a society where men hunt and women gather. The sex of an individual is generally apparent and recognized by the members of the society. Division of labor may also be based on gender in which member of one biological sex may perform tasks generally assigned to the opposite sex.

But there is a third category of sex, called intersexual (or hermaphroditic), in which individuals have elements of both sets of reproductive anatomy. In Western societies, such individuals are often assigned a sex at birth and then surgically altered to conform to that assignment. Even if exterior (visible) anatomy is altered, internal anatomy (e.g., a surgical female with internal testicles or a surgical male with ovaries) may be missed. In addition, hormonal traits that appear at puberty cannot be controlled. As a result, some individuals raised as one sex might manifest the opposite sex later in life, creating a great deal of emotional pain and confusion. Intersexual individuals in small societies are not altered to conform to some binary ideal but develop naturally, and in doing so, are often seen as special and esteemed members of that society.

Sexual preference

Sexual preference is not the same thing as biological sex. Although it is true that most individuals desire members of the opposite sex, there is, in fact, a great deal of variation in preference. This is true for many other mammals as well as humans.

One could classify human sexual preference as follows, remembering that biological sex is not always binary. Heterosexuals have sex exclusively with the opposite sex. Homosexuals have sex exclusively with the same sex. Bisexuals are nonexclusive and so can have sexual relations with either sex. A person might be asexual, choosing not to have sex with anyone. Sexual preference forms part of one's personal identity.

In Western societies, heterosexuality has been seen as the "ideal" while other preferences were "discouraged," although such attitudes are changing. As such, the expression of one's homosexual or bisexual preferences were and are often hidden. However, most other societies recognize that this range of variation is typical. To illustrate, males in some South Pacific island groups transition from being nonsexual as children, to homosexual in youth, to bisexual in early adulthood, to heterosexual after marriage. Ordinary behavior.

Gender

"Gender" is different from sex (e.g., Mascia-Lees and Black 2017). One's sex is generally defined by biology while gender is generally defined by the individual. Thus, gender is one's personal identity, their role in the society. Westerners commonly associate gender with sexual preference and while that often the case, there are many other genders, such as cross-dressers, transsexuals, people who never marry, and female "warriors" (e.g., Lang 1998). In the 1970s in the United States, women were generally expected to be "stay at home mothers" who did the housework and cooking (a stereotypic female gender). If a male were to fulfill that role, he would occupy a different gender (a "house" husband) but would not change sexual preference. Most societies embrace these differences but others, such as most Western societies, find them difficult to accept (this too is changing).

Gender selection

Gender selection by an individual has three major aspects: (1) recognizing one's own identity, (2) expression of that identity to others, and (3) the assumption of that gender role in society. Most (but not all) people will know their own identity. Expressing it may be quite difficult, especially if the society is disapproving of different genders. For example, not many male corporate executives would admit to being cross-dressers (transvestites).

While there are many potential genders, several stand out as visible to most people. "Transgenders" are people that identify themselves in a gender different from their biological sex, such as cross-dressers, and is independent of sexual preference. "Transsexuals" are those who have had their sex surgically changed to match their gender (not common in small societies). "Eunuchs" are males who have been castrated (having their testicles removed, damaged, or crushed; a worldwide practice) for a particular role, such as guarding a harem.

Chapter summary

The identity of a person is multilayered, including being a member of a variety of different groups. A person is first a member of a society and family and might be assigned a group identity by others, such as one based on race, ethnic groups, or subculture. Second, a person has a personal identity that is layered on group identity but is largely under the control of the individual. Such a personal identify may include sex, sexuality, and gender.

Sex is a biological classification based on reproductive anatomy (male or female) and the assignment of sex is quite important in societies that have a distinct division of labor based on sex. There is a third category of sex, called intersexual (or hermaphroditic), in which individuals have elements of both sets of reproductive anatomy. In Western societies, intersexual individuals may be surgically altered to be either male or female but in small societies they develop naturally and are often seen as special and esteemed members of that society.

Sexual preference is not the same thing as biological sex. Heterosexuals have sex exclusively with the opposite sex. Homosexuals have sex exclusively with the same sex. Bisexuals are nonexclusive. In Western societies, heterosexuality has been seen as the ideal while other preferences were discouraged and frequently hidden. However, most other societies recognize that this range of variation is typical.

Gender is different still, being one's personal identity, their role in the society. Gender selection by an individual has three major aspects: (1) recognition, (2) expression, and (3) the assumption of the gender role. The expression of one's gender may be quite difficult, especially if the society is disapproving of different genders. While there are many potential genders, several stand out as visible to most people, including transgenders, transsexuals, and eunuchs.

10 Religion, ritual, and knowledge

Religion and ritual commonly co-occur as cultural elements (e.g., Stein and Stein 2017) but are separate concepts. Most religion is ritualized but not all ritual is religious. Thus, the two are considered separately here.

Religion

Religion, in broad and general sense, is the belief in supernatural powers, beings, or forces. Religion is a cultural universal even though not all individuals are religious. Belief in the supernatural can be very general and unrelated to any formal "religion" and can manifest in a number of ways, such as concepts of luck, power, or magic.

A formal "religion" is a coherent set of specific beliefs about the supernatural and is based on faith (essentially a nonempirical science, see Chapter 1). Common examples of a formal religion include Christianity, Islam, and Judaism. All religions include an explanation of the world (cosmology), have practitioners (e.g., Priests, Imams, or Rabbis), and have ceremonies and rituals. Belief in an afterlife is a common constituent.

Each society has a religion and some have many. Large, multi-cultural societies, such as the United States, encompass many religions and one of the hallmarks of US society (and many others) is the freedom to practice whatever religion one wants to (recognizing that some organizations and individuals in US society are not so tolerant).

Small societies generally have a single religion practiced by all its members. As such, there are literally thousands of individual religions in the world, each believing theirs is the true one. Many societies do not separate religion from other aspects of culture, making everyday activities "religious." For example, the Navajo have no separate word for "religion" and everything they do is related to the maintenance of harmony in the universe.

General forms of religious belief

As noted, not all religious beliefs are part of formal religions and there are a number of general forms of religious behaviors and beliefs that can either stand alone or be incorporated into formal religions.

"Animism" is the belief that objects and entities in nature, such as clouds, mountains, and animals, including humans, are animated (energized) by distinct spirit beings. These spirit beings are concerned with, and so are "involved" in, most human activities. It is possible that the idea of humans being animated by spirits is the origin of the concept of the soul. Animism is typical of peoples who see themselves as a part of nature rather than superior to it (which is what most Westerners believe). Animism may be the first form of religious belief.

"Animatism" is the belief of the existence of cold and impersonal supernatural power, often found in societies where animism is practiced. Unlike animism, the power is neutral, does not take a particular shape or emotion, and can be used in any way (good or bad) by a knowledgeable person, such as a shaman. A common example of such a power is Mana, the power used in societies of the South Pacific. The "Force" of Star Wars movies is a fictional example of the same thing. Animatism is also part of the belief systems of industrial societies, manifesting as "luck," either good (such as the good luck of rabbit's feet) or bad, such as crossing paths with black cats, breaking mirrors, or having 13th floors in buildings. Both animism and animatism can be incorporated into more complex religions.

Many religions have deities, supernatural beings of some type that are considered sacred. Deities can take a number of forms. Those that are "physical" take either animal (zoomorphic) or human (anthropomorphic) form. Such beings may have originated in noncalendric times (recall the Dreamtime, see Chapter 3) but may still be active.

Many, probably most, religions include a number of deities, called "polytheism." These deities might be spirits of natural things such as mountains, rivers, or volcanos, or powerful animals, such as lions or bears. In some religions (think the ancient Greeks and Romans), there may be an assortment (or pantheon) of anthropomorphic Gods and Goddesses that reign over things such as the ocean, war, love, and the underworld. There may be one God in the pantheon that is supreme, such as Zeus in the ancient Greek religion.

Some religions worship a single deity as the creator and master of the universe, called "monotheism." This is the form that most Westerners are familiar with. But even in Christianity, there are subordinate deities, such as Satan.

Functions of religion

Religion and/or spiritual practices can provide a very positive framework to fulfill numerous social and psychological needs. First, religious cosmology explains the origin of the world and everything in it, including humans. This adds a structure to everyday life and explanation of the environment. Religion can explain death and so reduce the associated anxiety and provide a path for people to transcend the burdens of mortal existence. Religion can provide a moral and ethical compass, reinforce community values, and create a social hierarchy.

However, religion can also be used for purposes that are not so positive. Some religions, or radical interpretations of a religion, can be used as a justification for violence against people of other faiths. Much of the warfare seen in the world today is the result, at least in part, of conflict between religions.

Religious specialists

All societies have individuals that specialize in the guidance of the religious practices of others, such as Priests, Imams, Rabbis, or Shamans. These religious specialists hold specific rights to contact and influence supernatural beings and manipulate supernatural forces. They will have undergone special training and may display certain distinctive personality traits that make them particularly well suited to perform these tasks. Such specialists hold a special status in their society.

Most small societies have part-time religious specialist, commonly called a "shamans." The shaman may be able to influence or control the supernatural and may enter into an altered state of consciousness to contact and utilize a "hidden reality" in order to acquire knowledge and/or power and to help others. This hidden reality is commonly accessed through the use of hallucinogenic drugs or through the practice of deprivation, such as fasting for long periods so as to bring on visions. In addition to religious duties, it is common for the shaman to be the medical practitioner for the group as curing illness would usually involve religious actions.

Being a shaman could bring prestige, wealth, and an outlet for self-expression. However, if a shaman was consistently unsuccessful in getting results, they may lose their position to another. Also, if a shaman were to use their power for evil, they may be killed by the group. So, be careful!

Magic

"Magic" is a body of knowledge (not the illusion of Las Vegas "magic" shows) used to accomplish specific goals, with each undertaking having its own specific "recipe." To work, magic must include a component of supernatural power, generally animatistic in nature. Magic is closely aligned with religion and even medical treatments in small societies. Magic is one way to gain control over uncontrollable situations and can be used to obtain any number of desired results, such as to guarantee good crops, the fertility of livestock, the replenishment of hunted game, the prevention of accidents, to kill an enemy, to cure an illness, and much more. However, it must be done correctly to work.

Successful magic is similar to baking a cake. One must have all of the proper ingredients, in the proper amounts, added in the proper order, baked at the proper temperature, and for the proper amount of time. Deviations from the recipe will result in a bad cake. Magic follows the same rules, with the addition of the proper supernatural power in the right amount at the right time. If all this is done properly, the magic will work. If the magic fails, it must be because it was not done properly.

Magic can be divided into a number of types, but two are quite common. "Imitative magic" is when the desired result is imitated, and with the magic transferring the results to the target. A good example of this type of magic is the voodoo doll. Stick a pin in the doll and its pain will be transferred to the intended victim, but only if done properly and with the addition of supernatural power. "Contagious magic" is based on the principle of contagion. Something from the target, such as fingernail clippings or hair, is obtained and the magic applied to it. The desired result is then magically transferred to the target. People in many societies believe in such magic and closely guard their fingernail clippings, hair, and other items to avoid being victimized.

Ritual

"Ritual" is simply a specific or routine way of doing things that is generally repetitive and identifiable by others. Rituals may be quite simple and personal or may be culturally prescribed symbolic acts, ceremonies, or procedures designed to guide members of a community. Rituals also serve to convey information about social status and can help in calming tensions and integrating communities.

Some rituals are secular while others attempt to influence the supernatural. For example, a simple secular ritual might be one's morning activities in preparation for going to your Introduction to Cultural Anthropology class. Other simple rituals may attempt to invoke supernatural power, such as a baseball player kissing his cross necklace and pointing skyward for "luck" prior to batting. Still other simple rituals may be highly religious, such as daily prayer. Still other rituals can be highly complex and may be very religious, such as the Pope holding Mass.

Rites of passage

Other complex rituals involve "rites of passage": ritually moving from one state to another, such as adolescence to adult (a puberty ritual), uneducated to educated (a graduation), unmarried to married (a wedding), and alive to dead (a funeral). Such rites of passage rituals may be either secular or religious but might contain elements of both.

It is useful to consider rites of passage by breaking them down into three phases, called liminal stages: separation, transition, and incorporation. For example, a boy preparing for his puberty ceremony (or ritual) would first be separated from the other boys. He would then enter a transition phase in which he was neither a child nor an adult. Finally, he would be incorporated into his new state, that of being an adult. This process can be rather simple and quick to very complex and time consuming, depending on the society. Although Western societies do not have complex puberty rites, there are many other rites of passage that are practiced, such as marriage, school graduation, confirmation, retirement, and death.

Ritual cannibalism

Cannibalism is eating one's own species, in this case, humans eating humans. This is generally an uncomfortable topic and it is quite derogatory to be accused of cannibalism. There are a number of types of cannibalism, including criminal, emergency (eating human flesh to survive, such as the Donner Party), culinary (eating human flesh as part of the regular diet, no well documented examples), sociopolitical (to control a population, as in the ancient American Southwest), and ritual.

Ritual cannibalism is quite common and generally involves the consumption of small pieces of flesh as part of rituals designed to honor the dead, to gain power from an enemy, or for some other purpose. In eastern New Guinea, people would eat very small pieces of the deceased's brain as part of the funeral. In Madagascar, the uncle of a newly circumcised young man would eat the foreskin. Catholics, in a highly ritualized act, eat small wafers and wine or juice that, through the process of Transubstantiation, became the body and blood of Christ.

Funerary systems

Everybody dies and each society must have a system to the treatment of the body and soul of the dead, called a funerary system (Sutton 2021b). The details of treatment are generally dependent on social identities, including age, sex, gender, social position, ethnicity, and the like (e.g., Binford 1971). Here, a funerary system is defined (following Sutton 2021b) as having three components (cf. liminal stages): (I) pretreatment of the living; (II) mortuary treatment; and (III) commemorative behaviors (Figure 10.1).

The first aspect of a funerary system (I) is pretreatment, activities undertaken in preparation of a person for their death, the entry to the next stage of existence. This might include a variety of behaviors, such as caring for the terminally ill. Unless a death is unexpected, most societies will have some sort of pretreatment for the deceased, such as anticipatory grief, prayer vigils,

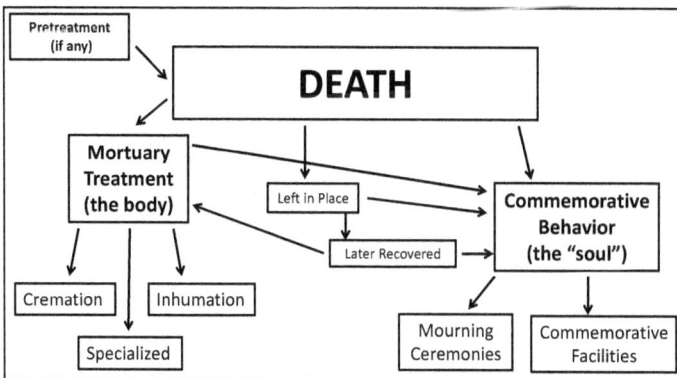

Figure 10.1 A general schematic of a funerary system (from Sutton 2021b: Figure 4.1).

ritual meals, placing someone in hospice, living with the dying, caring and preparing the person for death, the predeath dispersal of property, and/or the gathering of relatives.

The second aspect of a funerary system is the mortuary process (II), or the various practices, behaviors, and facilities that are involved in directly dealing with the physical body of the deceased. Some sort of mortuary process would be afforded to each member of a society, with initial and final phases. The initial mortuary treatment (IIa) involves the preparation of the body for the funeral, such as washing and dressing the body.

The final mortuary treatment (IIb) involves the burial, cremation, or mummification of the body. In some societies, such as in the South Pacific region, bodies are preserved by being dried over a fire and then placed back in their homes to remain part of the family. After a time, the bodies will be eventually be buried. Some past societies, such as the Ancient Egyptians, purposefully mummified their dead for the afterlife. Some societies may have specialized facilities (e.g., funeral homes) to deal with the mortuary process, and other specialized facilities (e.g., cemeteries) to place the dead.

The third part of the funerary system (III) is commemorative behavior, the various belief systems, practices, and facilities that are involved primarily with the afterlife, the remembrance of a person, and the management of their soul. Commemorative behaviors can be proximate to death, such as ceremonies at the funeral, erecting a grave marker, and making offerings or sacrifices. Commemorative behaviors occurring after the final mortuary treatment can occur over a considerable period of time and might include permanent memorials to a person (e.g., the Taj Mahal). Some such behaviors are simple, such as a visit by a relative to a gravesite, while others can be quite elaborate, such as the "Day of the Dead" events in Mexico.

Knowledge

All societies possess knowledge about their environment, both the living (biotic) and nonliving (abiotic) components. In Western societies, this knowledge is generally called "science" while in non-Western traditional societies, it is called "ethno-science" (Gragson and Blount 1999: vii), sometimes called folk science. Ethnoscience captures much of the overall knowledge of many small societies and includes information about a multitude of subjects, including plants, animals, forests, weather, geography, astronomy, and medicine. Such knowledge is often encoded into religious systems (e.g., Rappaport 1971, 1999).

All societies construct a system to classify the things in their environments. One society may classify animals based on morphology whereas another might classify them based on habitat. Thus, in the first system, a whale would be classified as being very different than a tuna (mammals and fish), while in the second, the two animals would be seen as similar (living in the ocean). The study of the classification, use, and know-ledge of the biotic environment is called "ethnobiology" (e.g., Albuquerque et al. 2014) and includes knowledge of plants ("ethnobotany") and animals ("ethnozoology"). Knowledge of the abiotic environment includes understandings of geog-raphy, soils, and meteorology. In addition, all societies recog-nize and maintain specific geographic places in the landscape (e.g., Feld and Basso 1996), as was noted in the discussion of the Dreamtime. A knowledge of soils and soil types would be critical for agriculturalists and knowing, predicting, and con-trolling the weather and climate is important in all societies, though most apparent in agricultural ones. Finally, everyone has an "ethnoastronomy," an understanding of the cosmos.

All societies also have medical knowledge, called "ethnomedicine" (e.g., Erickson 2008). Some of this know-ledge includes the setting of broken bones and the like but it mostly involves classification and use of plants, animals, and other substances for medical purposes, called "ethnopharmacology." The field also includes the knowledge and use of substances to alter one's reality (e.g., hallucinogenic drugs). In many societies, the people who specialize in medicine are often the same people who specialize in religion, and the two fields are often combined by a single practitioner.

One truth that emerges is that the Western world can learn a great deal from other societies. The wealth of knowledge, or intellectual property, encoded in all the religions and oral traditions of traditional societies has proved to be massive. Countless new medicines, foods, and industrial crops continue to be developed from traditional plant and animal sources. Agricultural practices are being reformed in many areas, due to the special knowledge of local people.

However, intellectual property rights remain an issue in regard to this knowledge (Posey 2001). It has been argued that traditional knowledge is being stolen without compensation to the holder of the knowledge, a sort of copyright or patent infringement. Many see this as an extension of Western colonial practices and a further exploitation of traditional peoples. Ways to deal with this issue, such as extending "copyright laws" to include unwritten traditions, are being proposed (Laird 2002).

Chapter summary

Religion is the belief in supernatural powers, beings, or forces and is a cultural universal. A formal "religion" is a coherent set of specific beliefs about the supernatural and is based on faith, such as Christianity, Islam, and Judaism. Each society has a religion and some have many. Small societies generally have a single religion practiced by all its members and so there are literally thousands of individual religions in the world, each believing theirs is the true one.

Animism is the belief that objects and entities in nature are animated (energized) by distinct spirit beings. Animatism is the belief of the existence of cold and impersonal supernatural power, often found in societies where animism is practiced. This power is neutral, does not take a particular shape or emotion, and can be used in any way (good or bad). Aspects of both animism and animatism can be incorporated into more complex religions.

Many religions have deities, supernatural beings of some type that are considered sacred. Deities can take a number of forms, such as animals (zoomorphic) or humans (anthropomorphic). Many religions are polytheistic, having a number of deities, while others are monotheistic, with one deity as the creator and master of the universe.

Religion can provide a very positive framework to fulfill numerous social and psychological needs. However, religion can also be used for purposes that are not so positive, such as to justify violence against people of other faiths.

All societies have individuals that specialize in the guidance of the religious practices of others, such as Priests, Imams, or Rabbis. Most small societies will have a part-time religious specialist, commonly called a shaman. The shaman may control the supernatural, and utilize a hidden reality of supernatural beings and powers in order to acquire knowledge, power, and to help others.

Magic is a body of knowledge involving the use of supernatural power and used to accomplish specific tasks. Magic is closely aligned with religion and even medical treatments in small societies. To be successful, magic must be done properly and if the magic fails, it must be because it was not done properly. Imitative magic is when the desired result is imitated, with the magic transferring the result to the target. Contagious magic is based on the principle of contagion, performing the magic on something from the target, then magically transferring desired result is to the target.

Ritual is simply a specific or routine way of doing things that is generally repetitive and identifiable. Some rituals are secular while others attempt to influence the supernatural. Other complex rituals involve rites of passage: ritually moving from one state to another, such as adolescence to adult (a puberty ritual), unmarried to married (a wedding ceremony), and alive to dead (a funeral).

Cannibalism is eating one's own species. There are a number of types of cannibalism, including criminal, emergency, culinary, sociopolitical, and ritual. Ritual cannibalism is quite common and generally involves the consumption of small pieces of flesh as part of rituals designed to honor the dead, to gain power from an enemy, or for some other purpose.

Each society has a funerary system, generally related to religion and imbued with ritual. Funerary systems have three parts, (I) pretreatment of the living to prepare for death, (II) mortuary treatment, preparation of the body for the funeral and the actual burial, cremation, or mummification, and (III) commemorative behaviors to treat the soul of the deceased and to soothe the living.

Finally, all societies have a body of unique knowledge. This knowledge includes an understanding of plants, animals, medicines, the cosmos, land management, and so much more. Western societies can learn a great deal from such societies. However, intellectual property rights remain an issue.

11 Expressive culture

Expression is something that is done by everyone, both as individuals and as societies. Expression can manifest as various kinds of play and art. Both play and art can be done for a variety of purposes and can have a number of important functions in a society.

Play

All mammals play and it has been said that "it is better to play than to do nothing." "Play" is an activity of some sort that is usually done for enjoyment or recreation. Play is commonly associated with children but all ages engage in play and in some cases, such as professional sports, it can be very serious. Every society has games of some sort and all recognize the importance of play, especially for children.

Play contains a number of important elements. Much of it is ritualized with specific rules and behavior with expectations of order and fairness. In addition, play usually has a temporal component, such as beginning and ending at specific times and spatial constraints, such as boundaries on a field or board. Play may be repeated, suspended, or resumed at any time. Finally, sufficient repetition can make certain play traditional. For example, the traditional game of lacrosse was borrowed from Native Americans in the southeastern United States.

Play can serve a number of important functions. Play is a way to train the body (e.g., coordination), to learn things, to communicate and socialize, to motivate and engage people, and to allow for the creation of alternative realities and the separation of the player from everyday life. Some play involves exercise, used to keep fit and as way to reduce stress.

Art

"Art" has a different meaning to both individuals and societies and some might even consider it a form of play. The ubiquity of art seems to reflect a basic human desire for harmony and balance and all societies have and appreciate art in its various forms. In general, categories of art include visual, verbal, musical, and performance.

Fundamentally, art is communication, to individuals, groups, or to the society as a whole. Such communication can be used to motivate political change, perhaps as propaganda, to provide a commentary on society, to reinforce cultural norms, or for psychological and healing purposes. Some art is used in ritual or as part of ceremonies, perhaps as music and/or rhythmic movement ("dances"), as a way to communicate with the supernatural as an aspect of religious belief, such as to maintain contact with the supernatural (see Figure 3.1). Other art, perhaps in the form of dress, decoration, or tattoos, may be used to visually announce one's status and/or membership in a social group. Art can also serve as entertainment or enjoyment (aesthetics). In some cases, graffiti could be seen as a form of folk art in Western societies.

Some art may have been used to enter into a mysterious or supernatural realm. In some cases, art may be hidden for some purpose, such as the Paleolithic cave art in France (e.g., the Lascaux site) (Figure 11.1). Other art may be placed to be obvious to those passing by, perhaps to mark territory.

Visual art

Visual art comes in a variety of types. Some is in the form of images draw on or painted on various surfaces such as paper, canvas, tree bark, and human skin (including the human body)

Figure 11.1 Paleolithic cave paintings in the Lascaux site in France (Wikimedia Commons).

Figure 11.2 An example of Inuit sculpture (photo by Caroline Léna Becker, Wikimedia Commons).

and is generally two-dimensional. Sculpture, a three-dimensional form, can be done in a variety of materials, including stone, ivory (Figure 11.2), metal, and wood. Other types of art include decorated woven cloth, clothing, and jewelry (Figure 11.3). In

Figure 11.3 An example of Massai decorative clothing (photo by Guillaume Tranquard, Wikimedia Commons).

many cases, this just reflects fashion, but it might also reflect status. The same is true for body adornment, such as piercings, tattoos, and scarification. For example, in Polynesian societies, body tattoos were used to communicate one's status, kinship identity, and personal identity.

Another form of visual art is rock art. Pictographs are figures painted on rock, petroglyphs are figures pecked into the rock, and geoglyphs are figures demarcated in the surface of the ground. One of the most famous sets of geoglyphs is the "Nasca Lines" in Peru (Figure 11.4).

Verbal art

The telling of stories, legends, tales, poetry, metaphor, rhyme, chants, drama, proverbs, jokes, puns, riddles, and tongue twisters

Figure 11.4 One of the geoglyphs at Nasca, Peru (Pixabay).

are all part of verbal art. Such communication is often for entertainment but it is also the way in which children are enculturated into their society and so is of critical importance.

"Oral tradition" (the term myth is avoided since it implies falsehood) is the unwritten stories, beliefs, and customs of a society, that are transmitted orally. It is through oral tradition that the history of a society, its culture, its religion, and its general knowledge is transmitted and reinforced. Oral tradition also serves as proxy experience and provides lessons in morality and behavior.

Musical art

Music is an art form whose medium is sound and silence, and is integral in all societies. It includes a nonverbal auditory component with elements of tonality, rhythm, pitch, a repetition of sounds and includes both song and musical instruments. The earliest known musical instruments, flutes and whistles, date from 42,000 years ago, but music itself must be much older.

Music can be strictly entertainment, created for self-expression, to build and maintain group solidarity (e.g., national anthems), or to maintain contact with the supernatural. Songs contain verbal components that can be used as communication of feelings, protest, to synchronize work as well as to pass the time.

Music can be utilized by particular minority or ethnic group express their plight to those in the larger majority. This provides the opportunity to communicate their dissatisfaction and possibly receive attention. Finally, Americans are obsessed with music, the vast majority of which are love songs, telling you Americans are obsessed with love.

Performance art

Performance art is generally associated with some dynamic action, such as dance. Performances can be varied, such as musical, acting, or recitation, and are generally done before an audience. Most, if not all, societies have some form of performance art, some done for entertainment, but with many being central to ceremonial activities.

Many ceremonial activities contain dynamic action, some by individuals and some by groups. For example, individual shamans will conduct actions to cure a sick person that will involve activity (e.g., chanting and/or rhythmic movement) and perhaps even paraphernalia. Many societies conduct ceremonies that involve groups of individuals performing a coordinated activity, often called "dances." For example, a "cast" of performers in costume may conduct a dramatic rendition of the cosmology (origin story) of a society. Another example is that of Puebloan societies in the American Southwest performing katsina ceremonies. Such ceremonies are extraordinarily important, are the responsibilities of moieties, and may involve as many as 50 performers.

Chapter summary

Expression, whether by individuals or societies, can manifest as play and/or art. Play is an activity of some sort that is usually done for enjoyment or recreation, and although commonly associated with children, all ages engage in play. Most play is ritualized and can serve a number of important functions, including communication, socialization, and the creation of alternative realities.

Art might be considered a form of play but fundamentally, it is communication. Art has a variety of functions, for entertainment, for political or social change, to reinforce cultural norms, or for psychological and healing purposes. Some art is used in ritual or as part of ceremonies. Other art may be used to visually announce one's status and/or membership in a social group.

Visual art, such as drawn or painted images, sculpture, or woven materials, may reflect a variety of meanings, including entertainment and religion. Rock art might represent spiritual images, or reflect a mysterious or supernatural realm. However, in many cases, the purpose of rock art is unknown.

Verbal art involves the recitation of stories for entertainment or enculturation. Oral tradition is the unwritten stories, beliefs, and customs of a society, and is how the general knowledge and traditions of a society is transmitted and reinforced. Oral tradition also serves as proxy experience and provides lessons in morality and behavior.

Musical art is a verbal (song) and nonverbal (instrumental) auditory experience. It can be for entertainment, to build and maintain group solidarity, to maintain contact with the supernatural, the communication of feelings or protest, to synchronize work, or to pass the time.

Performance art is generally some dynamic action, such as dance but may include music, acting, or recitation done before an audience. Performance art may be done for entertainment but it is also central to many ceremonial activities, some done by individuals and others by groups.

12 Change and development

That all things change is the one constant in the universe. Evolution is change and organisms change as they evolve, sometime fast sometimes slow. Culture and societies also change, a process called cultural evolution. Recall that UCE, the first coherent theory in anthropology, proposed that culture changed along a single line toward a European ideal. We know that is not the case, but it is still clear that culture evolves and societies change.

Although the mechanisms of cultural evolution are not fully understood, we do know that societies have to adjust to changes in both their natural and cultural environments, such as dealing with climate change, neighboring societies, or a pandemic. As traditional, and other, groups come into contact with larger societies and are forced to "develop" and enter a global system, they undergo major change. This change is a two-way street and impacts both the colonizer and the colonized; in effect, it impacts all of us in everything we do.

Change

All societies strive to adapt to their environment and as the environment changes, adjustments have to be made. This can be stressful and the archeological record of the Fifth World is full of past groups that failed to adapt. Pressures to change and manifest in a number of ways. The natural environment will change in both the short (weather) and long (climate) terms, and major changes will force major adaptations.

The cultural environment will also change in any number of ways. Populations may increase or decline or there may be foreign invasion. The membership of the society will change as people are born and die and new leaders will emerge. These things can lead to changing values, ideas, and/or cognitive systems.

Development and globalization may intrude, bringing with it a rapid pace of change. New technologies may appear that could completely alter life for traditional people (think of how computers and cell phones have altered Western societies). New trade goods might arrive and may then become "necessities." Demand for some material, such as "tourist" items, may completely reshape a traditional economy from food production to manufacturing, forcing the importation of food and a change in diet that would likely be less beneficial for the people. Missionaries may bring new religions, replacing traditional ones and altering cosmology, ritual, and ceremony. Tourism into these small societies might completely change their living patterns and conditions.

Adaptation

The vast majority of adaptation is cultural, there are only a few short-term minor biological adaptations such as sweating when you are hot. Each society has a unique cultural system, and that system is used adapt to changing conditions. Some cultural changes can be very small and even daily, such as changing what is eaten for dinner. If changed often enough, the new foods may become traditional.

Each society manages its environment through a variety of means (Table 12.1) and as conditions change, management methods must also change (Sutton and Anderson 2014). People have organizations and methods to control and manipulate the environment, either directly or indirectly. Examples of direct manipulation is damming a river and changing its flow to agricultural fields or clearing track of forest to plant grass.

Table 12.1 Examples of environmental control

Method	General principle	Scale	Examples
Environmental manipulation			
Active	Actual hands-on purposeful modification	Large, as in landscapes	– Alteration of natural water systems for irrigation – Clearing of large tracts of forest for agricultural fields
Passive	Ritual activities to effect control and change	Large, as in landscapes	– Stewardship of areas to maintain their power, such as for the Dreamtime
Resource management			
Active (light to moderate)	Purposeful alteration of a resource to achieve a result	Small, generally individual resources	– Pruning specific plants to enhance production
Active (intensive)	Purposeful alteration of a resource to achieve a result	Small, but intense focus on an individual species	– Agricultural domestication of a species, such as corn or cattle
Passive	Ritual activities to effect control and change	Small, focus on specific need	– Giving thanks to a species (e.g., deer) for allowing themselves to be killed

Source: Table by author.

An example of indirect manipulation is a system of supernatural ceremonies and rituals to ensure the continuance of harmony, such as the system used by Indigenous Australians to maintain the Dreamtime.

Each society also manages its resources (see Table 12.1). This can be done through active methods, such as pruning plants or breeding them to the point of domestication. Passive methods might include thanking hunted animals for their sacrifice to ensure continued hunting success.

Invention and innovation

"Invention" is the discovery or development of any new idea, method, or device while "innovation" is the modification of, or addition to, an existing idea, method, or device. Everything anyone has or uses was invented or innovated for some reason at some point in time. Thus, this is a major factor in cultural change.

Diffusion

Diffusion is the spread of ideas, customs, or practices from one society to another, either through exchange or immigration. Societies in close proximity may have considerable diffusion between them. Although diffusion can account for some change, it does not account for all since independent invention also occurs (recall diffusionism from Chapter 2).

In most small societies with relatively little contact with others, diffusion would take place but probably fairly slowly. Today, rapid travel, trade, and complex communication can all help diffusion occur at a rapid pace.

Colonization

"Colonization" occurs when one society occupies the territory of another and assumes control of that territory and of the resident population. The original society might be acculturated into the new one (ethnocide), or killed (genocide), or they may be pushed out, often by force, and have to adjust to a new natural and cultural environment. If the colonized survive, they will suffer subjugation and suppression of their practices and beliefs and to be forced to change people's roles, such as women losing status in the "new" society. They will also lose their sovereignty and cultural identity. These impacts are generically called "colonialism," and this is the struggle of most Fourth World groups to this day.

Acculturation

"Acculturation" is people or societies adopting portions of the culture of another. For example, immigrants to the United States would typically voluntarily acculturate, although it may be a slow process and they may retain their identity as an ethnic group (see Chapter 3). Indigenous societies that come into contact with more dominant societies are often forced to acculturate. As a result, the people in such societies are left in despair and poverty and have great difficulty in surviving in their "new" society. If acculturation is total, it is called "assimilation."

Ethnocide and genocide

Forced acculturation (and assimilation) can also result in the destruction of the original society even if their members physically survive, a process called "ethnocide." In ethnocide, a society's language, religion, subsistence base, and other systems are suppressed, destroyed, and replaced by those of the conqueror to make the indigenous society suitable for exploitation. This "ethnoforming" is akin to the concept of terraforming, the remaking of the environment of a new planet to be suitable for colonization. Ethnocide is often the intentional policy of the dominant society (think of the United States policies toward Native Americans in the 1800s) but is also sometimes accomplished by other groups, such as missionary programs to "save" primitive people and raise them up to "civilization" or convert them to the "true religion."

"Genocide" is the physical extermination of one society or ethnic group by another, either as a deliberate act or as the incidental outcome of activities carried out by one group with little regard for their impact on others. For example, the unintentional introduction of crowd diseases (e.g., smallpox) into Native American populations by Europeans after 1492 resulted in the death of many millions of people with little effort to mitigate the effects.

There are many examples of genocide, sometimes called "ethnic cleansing." The most well-known examples include the Armenians during World War One and the Jews during World War Two. More recent examples include the Cambodian genocide (1975–1979), the Bosnian genocide (1992–1995), the Rwandan genocide (1994), and the ongoing genocides in the Darfur, the Middle East, and Myanmar.

In some cases, two or more societies that have been largely destroyed by ethnocide and/or genocide may coalesce to form a new society, a process called "ethnogenesis." An example of this latter process is the Seminole, formed in the mid-1800s from survivors of the Creek people of Georgia and runaway African slaves who fled into Florida (then under the control of Spain) to escape the Americans.

Development

"Development" is the process by which societies become connected to the World System and acquire some of the characteristics of contemporary industrialized societies, such as resource exploitation, creation of contemporary infrastructure, and trade. Development is related to colonization and is sought by many Third World countries. However, to most of the Fourth World people in those countries, development is a code word for acculturation and ethnocide. Indigenous people are often seen as being "in the way" of development and have few rights and little power to resist.

Development is accomplished through the powerful industrialized nations that control the World System. Both soft power (diplomacy, media, propaganda) and hard power (military and economic) are employed. In the absence of government control, private companies often (and illegally) use hard power to exploit resources with resulting negative consequences to Fourth World groups, such the murder of native people protesting deforestation in the Amazon.

In addition to the impacts on traditional peoples, development is not without its environmental consequences. Many traditional agricultural systems have operated in a stable, renewable, and productive way for millennia. But to make them more productive, traditional practices have been replaced by Western industrialized agriculture with its chemicals, mechanical labor, and resulting pollution. While production is increased in the short-term, the environmental impacts are detrimental and long-lasting. Examples of this include the replacement of the traditional Chinese and Ancient Egyptian agricultural systems.

Developmental intervention can also alter attitudes and classificatory systems. For example, in the past when locusts appeared in East Africa, people viewed them as food, welcoming their presence. Today, Westerners have convinced those same people that locusts are pests, not to be eaten but to be killed by pesticides. So, now, poisons are used to control locusts, poisons that also impact grain crops, reducing the overall food available and facilitating famines.

Reactions to imposed change

Colonization and development are usually resisted by traditional peoples. Resistance can vary from open warfare to efforts at revitalization. In the United States, a number of wars were fought with Native Americans resisting European and American encroachment and colonization. In other cases, such as in Mexico, Native peoples rebelled against the already established Spanish authorities. In both cases, Native peoples survived the conflicts and continue to be oppressed.

Another reaction to imposed change is to try to revitalize the affected society, called a "revitalization movement." A good example of this is the "Ghost Dance" of 1870 and 1890, undertaken to revitalize Native American societies. The 1870 effort was moderately successful and the 1890 effort failed. Nevertheless, the Ghost Dance is still performed by some Native American groups. Another example is the "cargo cult": a complex of ceremonies and magic undertaken by groups in the South Pacific to bring back the Western foods and material goods they had enjoyed during the occupation of their islands during World War Two and taken away when the military left the islands.

Other reactions to change seem more practical. During the European colonization of Australia, indigenous people congregated around ranches (called stations in Australia) to work and obtain food. Some of the stations later became the focus of aboriginal reservations whose people lived on government benefits. Beginning in the 1970s, some aboriginal people moved away from the stations back to their traditional lands to practice their traditional lifestyle and reacquire their sovereignty; an undertaking called the "Outstation Movement" (Myers and Peterson 2016). A number of Inuit families in Canada have done the same thing. Today, much of the resistance of Native peoples is focused on using the legal systems of their respective countries to address their grievances.

People moving

Another method to deal with change due to a host of issues, is to move. "Migration" is the movement of a group of people from one place to another to establish a new home. Migrations can happen for a variety of reasons, including poor living conditions, warfare, violence, and climate change. If a group migrates, it is usually to a place where other people already live, potentially creating problems. An example of this is the English moving to North America seeking religious freedom, only to become colonizers to the detriment of the Native Americans.

"Diaspora" is the movement, often forced, of segments of a population into a new area without replacing the original inhabitants. Perhaps the largest and most tragic diaspora was the slave trade bringing Africans to the Americas. Other diasporas have happened due to persecution, genocide (e.g., the Jews to Palestine), or famine (e.g., the Irish to the United States).

Climate change migration

"Climate change migration" is a relatively new and increasingly important issue across the world (e.g., Palinkas 2020). As the climate changes, impacted people are beginning to move to more favorable areas, becoming climate refugees. An earlier example of this phenomenon was the movement of people out of the American Midwest in the 1930s due to drought, known as the "dust bowl." A contemporary example is that a prolonged drought in Central America due to climate change is compelling people to migrate north to the United States, creating a major political issue in the United States.

Rising sea levels will force the movement of people away from the coast as cities, such as Miami, begin to flood (Goodell 2017). In the Arctic, Native Inuit groups are having their coastal villages and cemeteries destroyed by erosion due to sea level rise. Sea level rise is also in the process of inundating some of the low-lying Island Nations in the South Pacific Ocean, and will force people to abandon entire countries. In United States, hurricanes in the southeast and wildfires in the west are forcing people to relocate.

Chapter summary

Change (evolution) is a constant in environments, individuals, and societies. Change may happen slowly while other change is rapid, even sudden. Although the mechanisms of cultural evolution are not fully understood, societies do have to adjust to changes in both their natural and cultural environments. Changes in the natural environment might force people to move, to alter their subsistence, or even disappear. Changes in the cultural environment might result in population growth, foreign invasion, or the emergence of new leaders, all of which can then change values, ideas, and/or cognitive systems. Development may bring rapid change, such as the introduction of new technologies, trade goods, religions, and foods. People and societies have to adapt to change and most adaptation is done by culture (as opposed to biological change).

Each society manages its environment through a variety of means, such as direct or passive control of resources and manipulation of the environment, and through organization and social systems. Invention and innovation also play a role and these ideas and items can diffuse into other societies through a variety of means.

Colonization occurs when one society occupies the territory of another and either forces them to acculturate, kills them, or forces them to move. Forced acculturation can result in ethnocide, the destruction of the original society even if their members physically survive. It may also result in genocide, the physical extermination of the society.

Development, related to colonialism, is the process by which societies become connected to the World System to have their resources utilized largely by contemporary industrialized societies. Development is accomplished through both soft power (diplomacy, media, propaganda) and hard power (military and economic). In the absence of government control, private companies may also use such power, impacting traditional societies. In addition, development impacts the environment through habitat description and the replacement of traditional systems with Western ones.

Colonization and development may be resisted in a number of ways, including warfare, rebellion, and revitalization. In some cases in fairly recent times, traditional peoples may simply return to their lives away from Westerners. Another method to deal with colonization, and a host of other issues, is to move. Voluntary movement, migration, may alleviate one problem but cause another in the host region. Involuntary movement of people, diaspora, would have its own set of problems.

13 Applied anthropology

Through anthropology, we have learned a great deal about humans, their societies, practices, and customs. We understand that societies change, know at least some of the mechanisms of such change, and can begin to anticipate how societies can, or cannot, adjust to stress. What do we do with this knowledge? The field of applied anthropology deals with the application of anthropological knowledge to real world issues, to solve practical problems, to advocate for societies with little voice themselves, and the help shape governmental policies.

Applied anthropology was originally focused on advising governments about programs of directed cultural change and in solving practical problems through anthropological techniques. More recently, the scope of it has expanded and became more engaged and now, ideally, the work is done in collaboration and solidarity with indigenous societies.

How do anthropologists apply their knowledge? Recall that anthropology is supposed to be nonjudgmental and accepting of all cultural practices. So, when do we have the right to intervene in another society? At what level? Who makes those decisions? This is an ethical conundrum.

Here, three simple approaches to the complex application of anthropological knowledge are defined. These are (1) detached, (2) project-specific, and (3) proactive.

The detached approach

The "detached approach" is to not to do any applied anthropology. The argument is that although we do know a great deal about other societies, we do not yet know enough to make sound decisions about intervention. It is similar to the medical advice of "first, do no harm." Practitioners of this approach argue that we first need to do more research, gain additional knowledge, and to learn from the attempts of others who do applied anthropology. At some point, application of anthropological knowledge and expertise might be warranted. This approach does not appear to be very widely held.

The project–specific approach

The "project-specific" approach follows the idea that even though we do not yet have a complete understanding of societies and their contexts, various projects are going to impact them whether anthropologists are involved or not. Thus, it is better to do what we can to mitigate the impacts than to do nothing. Mistakes will be made, to be sure, but hopefully some good will come of it.

Most of the applied anthropology that is done is project-specific, often mandated by governmental agencies in advance of their projects. If there is a project that is going to impact native groups, governments will hire anthropologists to work with the groups, to identify impacts, and to propose and implement migration measures. Even though it is the developer (government or private) that usually pays for this work, anthropologists always advocate for the interests of the impacted groups.

There are other kinds of project-specific studies. For example, most of the ethnography and archaeology done in the United States today is project-specific, conducted under the umbrella of Cultural Resource Management (CRM). Forensic anthropologists may be called upon to help investigate criminal cases, including genocides. Finally, the military may hire anthropologists to assist with their relationships with other societies, such as in Afghanistan.

The proactive approach

Using a "proactive approach," some anthropologists actively seek to implement changes that they see as being beneficial or to change practices that they view as harmful. This is generally done outside of, and often in conflict with, governments since it is often the governmental policies themselves that are being challenged. It is common for advocates to directly work with, and advocate for, indigenous societies.

A good example of the proactive approach is the effort to stop the practice of female circumcision, sometimes called female genital cutting (FGC) or female genital mutilation (FGM). This practice, conducted worldwide, involves the surgical removal of the clitoris, ostensibly to reduce sexual desire in women (a form of control over women) although some groups see the clitoris as being "male" and so must be removed to validate the person as "female." The general problem is that the "surgery" is often done using just a razorblade, and can result in severe blood loss and sometimes even death. The United Nations has called for the cessation of the custom and some anthropologists are actively trying to stop it by working with groups that practice it.

This issue begs the question about intervention (as per the detached approach). Who decides what to change? When? How? What about the wishes of the affected society? What customs qualify for intervention? How does this approach interface with the traditional anthropological philosophy of cultural relativism? Should anthropologists intervene if a society has funerary practices where women lose a finger or cut their hair? What about food habits, such as eating insects or dogs? What about small-scale warfare? What about human rights violations or even genocide? Where do we draw the line? Certainly in the latter two cases, but there are no easy answers.

Chapter summary

We have learned a great deal about culture and society. Should we use that knowledge to address real world issues, to solve practical problems, or to advocate for societies with little voice themselves? Do we know enough to help them without harming them? How can we reconcile intervention with cultural relativism? These are difficult questions and there are a number of approaches in applied anthropology.

Three basic approaches to applied anthropology can be defined. The detached approach is to not to do any applied anthropology following the argument that we do not yet know enough. The project-specific approach follows the idea that societies will be impacted by projects whether anthropologist are involved or not. Thus, it is better to do what we can to mitigate the impacts than to do nothing. The proactive approach seeks to actively implement changes that are seen as beneficial or harmful, often in conflict with government policies.

But do anthropologists have the right to intervene in the affairs of other societies? What are the ethics of who decides what, when, where, and how? What about cultural relativism? Thee seem to be some obvious cases that require intervention, such as genocide, but what about the myriad of other cultural practices? There are no easy answers.

Glossary

Acculturation one society adopting the culture of another. Indigenous societies that come into contact with more dominant societies are often forced to adapt quickly to a new way of life, resulting in the abandonment of native languages, religious beliefs, or social practices

Achieved status or rank a status or rank obtained though one's own actions or ability

Actual behavior the behavior actually seen, sometimes different from the ideal behavior expected by a society (see ideal behavior)

Adaptation modification of the body, species, or society in response to changing environmental conditions

Affinal relatives those related by marriage

Age grades a group of people of the same basic age that pass through a number of categories as the age

Agency the power and ability of an individual to make their own choices

Animism the belief that objects and entities in nature, such as clouds, mountains, and animals, are animated (energized) by distinct spirit beings

Animatism The belief of the existence of impersonal supernatural power. Such power is neutral and can be used in any manner (good or bad) by a skilled person; called mana in the South Pacific and the "force" in Star Wars

Anthropology the study of humans (biology, culture, language, past and present, etc.)

Applied anthropology the use of anthropological knowledge and methods to solve practical problems, often for a specific purpose (see Detached approach, Project-specific approach, and Proactive approach)

Archaeology the anthropological study of past (Fifth World) societies through the study of their remains

Arraigned marriages the type of marriage that was arraigned by the family, such as with royalty

Art a form of expressive culture, including visual, verbal, musical, performance forms

Ascribed status or rank a status or rank that is assigned, such as by birth or inheritance

Assimilation the process by which people are completely acculturated by a society. If forced upon a society, it would result in ethnocide

Authority the backing of the society to exert power

Band level of political complexity in which a society has a small population, lacks formal leaders, and in which the family is the primary socio-political and economic unit

Barter an exchange system involving two or more parties negotiate a direct exchange of one trade good for another, can use money, personal supply and demand

Benedict, Ruth a pioneering Anthropologist who studied Native peoples in the American Southwest and conducted the famous personality study of the Japanese during World War Two

Bilateral descent descent figured through both the mother's and father's side

Biological anthropology the anthropological investigation of human biology, evolution genetics, and primate ancestors

Black market the secret exchange of various goods or services done to avoid law, regulation, taxation, monitoring, or auditing

Boas, Franz the Anthropologist that worked extensively in the Northwest Coast of North America and developed the theory of Historical Particularism

Bridewealth (aka brideprice) a payment of some sort to the family of the bride to compensate for her leaving her family

Cannibalism eating one's own species. Several basic types, including ritual (fairly common), emergency (extreme circumstances), culinary (as a regular part of the diet, none documented), or sociopolitical (to exercise control of a group)

Cargo cult a revitalization movement undertaken to attract material goods, such as were seen in World War Two

Caste system a form of stratification that is often based on birthright, has no mobility, and is often associated with a profession

Chiefdom a level of political complexity in which a society has a relatively large population, permanent settlements, some central authority, and a stratified social structure, but no formal state institutions

Chinampa a small field constructed within or on a body of water

Circumcision (female) a body alteration in which some or all of the external female genitalia is removed. This practice is also known as female genital mutilation

Circumcision (male) a body alteration in which the foreskin of the penis is removed, associated with puberty rituals

Clan An extended unilineal kinship group, often consisting of several lineages, whose members claim common descent from a remote ancestor, usually legendary or cosmological

Class system form of stratification that is often based on economics and/or other factors and has mobility

Climate change migration the movement of people from one place to another due to the impacts of climate change, such as sea-level rise or drought

Coercion the use of force to exert power

Cognition the way in which information from the senses (perception) is processed and interpreted, including classification systems, decision-making, and planning

Cognitive linguistics the idea that people think in their language and that as such, their thought is limited to concepts present in that language

Collateral relatives consanguineal relatives not related in a direct line (e.g., uncles and aunts)

Colonialism the domination of and exploitation of small societies by (mostly) Western powers. Often thought of as a past phenomenon but it remains an issue

Colonization when one society occupies the territory of another and assumes control of that territory

Consanguineal relatives those related by blood

Consumption that part of an economic system in which goods or services are consumed, thus creating a need for continued production and exchange

Contagious magic based on the principle of contagion, the magic is applied to something related to the target, such as fingernail clippings, to transfer the result to the target

Cosmology an explanation for the origin of the universe and all this is in it

Cross-cousins children of opposite sex sibling of parent

Crow kinship system unilinear, mirror image of the Omaha system, with cross-cousins on the paternal side being merged with the parental generation

Cultural anthropology the anthropological study of extant (living) groups, typically using participant observation

Cultural appropriation the use of customs, traits, or imagery of a society by an outsider for some purpose, generally to the detriment of the original society

Cultural ecology the study of the cultural aspects of human interaction with the environment

Cultural loss the abandonment of an existing practice or trait

Cultural materialism a practical, rather simplistic functionalist approach to anthropology, with a focus on the specific how(s) and why(s) of culture

Cultural personality the "personality" of a society, generally reflecting its morality and norms

Cultural relativism the study of society without any attempt to show scientifically that one is "better" than another, societies are interpreted nonjudgmentally

Cultural universal a trait present in all societies, such as kinship or marriage

Culture learned and shared behavior in humans, including socially transmitted ideas, values, and how one views the world. Culture is used to make sense of experience and to generate appropriate behavior

"a" culture see society

Culture shock the stress that results from having to suddenly adjust to a new culture

Custom a trait practiced by a certain society, often unique to that society

Darwin, Charles the author of "The Origin of the Species" that detailed natural selection and evolution

Deity a supernatural being of some sort, might be in animal form (zoomorphic) or human form (anthropomorphic)

Demography the structure of a population, distributions of age and sex, ethnicity, professions and other cultural traits, incidence of disease

Detached approach in applied anthropology the idea that anthropological knowledge should not be applied to real world situations since we do not yet know enough to do so

Descent groups the way each society organizes its members along kinship lines

Diaspora the movement of segments of a population into a new area without replacing the original inhabitants, due to a variety of factors such as persecution, genocide, slavery, or famine

Division of labor specific tasks assigned to people based on sex, age, gender, and the like

Diffusion the spread of ideas, customs, or practices from one society to another

Diffusionism the theoretical approach that most things were invented once and diffused from those places, downplays independent invention as a source of traits

Division of labor the assignment of tasks based on some factor such as sex, gender, or age or in some societies, by education, status, or ethnicity

Divorce the termination of a marriage

Domestication a process by which organisms and/or landscapes are "controlled"; in agriculture, domestication means that the genetic makeup of an organism is purposefully altered by humans to their advantage

Dowry a payment of some sort to the family of the groom to compensate for his "loss"

Dreamtime the cosmology of the Indigenous Australians; the time before people when the world and all that is in it was created

Egalitarian informal inequality generally based on sex, age, ability, etc.

Emic the view of a society from the inside, their view of themselves (also see etic)

Empirical science knowledge system based on tangible data observable by other scientists ("hard" data, testable, reproducible)

Enculturation the process by which the young are indoctrinated into a society's natural and human-made environment along with a collective body of ideas about the self and others

Endogamy the rule that you must marry someone from within your group

Environment the natural or cultural surroundings within which a society interacts

Eskimo kinship system bilateral, emphasis on nuclear family, same system as used by most people in the United States

Ethics an understanding of right and wrong based on the morality defined by a society

Ethnic group people from other societies within a large society who collectively and publicly identify themselves as a distinct group based on various cultural features such as shared ancestry and common origin, language, customs, and traditional beliefs

Ethnicity the expression of ideas held by an ethnic group

Ethnoastronomy the classification and beliefs of a traditional society about the cosmos, planets, stars, and constellations

Ethnobiology the classification and beliefs of a traditional society about the biotic (living) environment

Ethnobotany the classification and beliefs of a traditional society about plants in their environment

Ethnocentrism the view that one's own group is superior to other groups

Ethnocide the destruction of a society due to contact with another

Ethnogenesis the formation of a new group from segments or remnants of other groups

Ethnographic present understanding of a society as it was at the time the information about it was collected, rather than present time

Ethnography the study of a particular group at a particular time

Ethnology the comparative study of culture

Ethnopharmacology the classification and use of substances in medicine

Ethnomedicine the practice of medicine in a traditional society

Ethnoscience knowledge possessed by a traditional society in a variety of disciplines, such as ethnobotany, ethnomedicine, ethnopharmacology, ethnozoology, and the like

Ethnotourism tourists visiting traditional societies and paying to be hosted and to "live with the natives"

Ethnozoology the classification and beliefs of a traditional society about animals in their environment

Etic the view of a society from the outside, such as an anthropologist's view of what indigenous people are doing (also see emic)

Eunuchs a gender category of males who have been castrated for a particular role

Evolution change (specific disciplines have more specific definitions)

Exchange that part of an economic system in which goods or services are moved around in the system by various means

Exogamy the rule that you must marry someone from outside your group

Expressive culture the means by which people express themselves, such as through art, music, and literature

Extended family generally seen as a large set of relatives, such as grandparents, aunts and uncles, parent, and children, all living together

Family broadly, a group of relatives related by blood, marriage, or adoption

Fictive kin unrelated people referred to by kinship terms, such as those considered family for some reason, such as Godparents

Fifth World refers to past societies known mostly through archaeology

Fission-fusion when a group periodically splits-up and later reforms, such a seasonal pattern of regional bands splitting into small local bands in the winter and reforming back into regional bands during the summer

Folkways minor and informal rules that if violated, result in minor sanctions, such as an expression of displeasure

Foragers a term commonly applied to small hunter-gatherer groups

Fourth World refers to indigenous societies without their own state living within modern countries.

Functionalism the theory developed by Bronislaw Malinowski that how a society functioned was the key to its understanding

Garden a small agricultural plot, tilled by hand

Gathering the collection of relatively small and nonmobile resources, such as wild plants, small land fauna, and shellfish

Gender how one identifies oneself, one's role in society. Has three major aspects; identity (one's view of oneself), expression (manifestation of identity to others), and assumption of one's gender role in society

Genocide the physical extermination of one society or ethnic group by another, either as a deliberate act or as the accidental outcome of activities carried out by one group with little regard for their impact on others

Gestures body motions used to convey messages

Ghost Dance a revitalization movement intended to reinvigorate Native American societies

Globalization the increasing interdependence of societies on others across the planet

Grammar the entire formal structure of a language including morphology and syntax

Hawaiian kinship system bilateral and generational

Hidden behavior behaviors that people would prefer that other people not know about, such as bathroom habits, certain sexual activities, or unethical activities

Historical linguistics the study of the history of languages, where they originated, when they moved, and why they moved

Historical particularism the theory, promoted by Franz Boas, that societies developed (evolved) based on their own particular history and situation

Holistic the recognition that a system (e.g., anthropology) is interconnected and that all the parts have to be considered in analysis

Horticulture low-intensity agriculture involving relatively small-scale fields, plots, and gardens; food raised primarily for personal consumption rather than for trade or a central authority, no supplemental labor

Household the primary residential unit of a family and the center of economic production, consumption, child rearing, and shelter

Hunters and gatherers groups that make their *primary* living from the exploitation of "wild" resources

Hunting actively looking for, killing, butchering, and consuming animals

Incest marriage or sexual relationships with close members of one's family, specific definitions vary by society but always includes the nuclear family

Ideal behavior the behavior encouraged and expected by a society but not necessarily the actual behavior seen (see actual behavior)

Indigenous people in their original homelands, even if now occupied by others, for example in North America, Native Americans are indigenous while Europeans are immigrants

Identity the assignment of one's place or role in a society, may be self-identified or ascribed by others

Imitative magic the type of magic that imitates the results on something, such as a voodoo doll, the transfer the results to the real target

Indigenous Australian Section Kinship System very complex system based on moieties, geography (sections), and ritual responsibilities

Inequality differential access to resources, power, wealth, etc.

Infanticide the intentional killing of infants for a variety of reasons

Innovation is the modification of, or addition to, an existing idea, method, or device

Intensive agriculture large-scale agriculture often involving the use of animal labor, equipment, and water diversion techniques, production of a surplus to feed specialists

Invention the discovery or development of any new idea, method, or device

Iroquois kinship system unilinear, same sex siblings of the parent are called by the same term as the parent and their children are siblings

Irrigation the purposeful diversion of water from its natural course onto agricultural fields

Kinship the system by which one figures one's family relationships

Language system of communication using sounds, gestures, or marks that are put together in according to a set of rules that result in meanings that are intelligible to all who share that language

Laws formal rules that if violated, result in serious sanction such as fines, incarceration, or death

Lexicon a specialized terminology used for some purpose, such as in a profession (like anthropology!)

Lineage a unilineal kinship group descended from a common ancestor or founder where relationships among members can be traced genealogically

Lineal relatives those related in a direct line, parent, grandparents, great grandparents, and the like

Linguistics the study of (human) language, including descriptive (the study of syntax and grammar), historical (the way languages change over time), and social aspects (see sociolinguistics)

Magic a body of knowledge plus supernatural power used to accomplish specific aims

Malinowski, Bronislaw the person that developed the theory of functionalism and the technique of participant observation

Market an exchange system that is impersonal, relies on general supply and demand, and requires money

Marriage the sanctioned union between two or more people that establishes rights and obligations between them and their children

Matrilineal descent descent figured through the mother's side

Matrilocal residence the postmarital residence pattern where a newlywed couple lives with or near the wife's family

Mead, Margaret a pioneering Anthropologist who studied people in Samoa and conducted the famous sex studies

Metaphor a phrase whose meaning dependent on previous cultural knowledge

Migration the movement of people from one place to another, generally the result of displacement due to poor living conditions, warfare, violence, or climate change

Milch pastoralism the production of milk as the major pastoral product, generally combined with blood to make a food

Moiety a organization of two (only two) groups of related clans, membership unchanging

Money anything agreed to by the society to use in an exchange system, such as salt, shells, stones, beads, feathers, fur, bones, teeth, paper, and most recently, cryptocurrencies

Monogamy the type of marriage in which there are two partners

Monotheism the belief in only one supremely powerful divinity as creator and master of the universe

Morality the difference between good and evil, as defined by each society

Mores informal but important rules that if violated, results in major sanctions such as being ostracized from the group

Morpheme the smallest units of sound that carry meaning

Morphology (linguistic) the study of the patterns or rules of word formation in a language

Multicultural the presence of a number of ethnic groups within a larger society, such as the many groups within the United States

Multilinear Cultural Evolution the idea that societies evolve along many lines

Mutualism a relationship between two species in which they both directly benefit

Neolocal residence the postmarital residence pattern where a newlywed couple establishes a residence away from their families

Nomads another term for pastoralists

Nonempirical science the system of learning in which data need not be empirical, testable, or repeatable, such as visions

Nuclear family the immediate family, parents and children living together in a household

Omaha kinship system unilinear, same sex siblings of the parent are called by the same term as the parent with the maternal cross-cousins being elevated to the parental generation and given the same terms

Oral tradition the unwritten stories, beliefs, and customs of a society, transmitted orally

Outstation movement the Indigenous Australian movement away from the outstations (ranches) so as to revitalize their culture

Paralanguage specific voice effects that accompany speech and contribute to communication, such as crying, laughing, signing, grunting, moaning

Parallel cousins the children of the same sex sibling as the parent, such as mother's sister's children

Participant observation the extended on-location research to gather detailed and in-depth information on a society's customary ideas, values, and practices through participation in its collective social life

Pastoralism the herding, breeding, consumption, and use of managed or domesticated animals, to the general exclusion of plants

Patrilineal descent descent figured through the father's side

Patrilocal residence the postmarital residence pattern where a newlywed couple lives with or near the husband's family

Patterned marriages the type of marriage in which there is an agreement to exchange partners, such as between villages

Perception information obtained by the senses, such as sight, sound, smell, taste, or touch

Personality the distinctive way a person thinks, feels, and behaves (also see cultural personality)

Persuasion the use of negotiation and/or compromise to exercise power

Phoneme distinct units of sound

Phratry an organization of more than two groups of clans, membership flexible

Phonology the study of the production, transmission, and reception of speech sounds.

Physical anthropology see biological anthropology

Piercing a body alteration in which the flesh is pierced for the insertion of some item

Play an activity done for enjoyment or recreation, although some "play" is very serious, such as professional sports

Politics the process of decision-making. It is an aspect of social organization that allocates and distributes power and authority in a society and the way that power is distributed and embedded in society; the means by which a society creates and maintains social order, to determine who gets what, when, and how

Polity an entity (e.g., society) with an independent political system

Polyandry a marriage in which the female has multiple husbands

Polygamy the type of marriage where there are multiple partners (see polyandry and polygyny)

Polytheism the belief in several gods and/or goddesses, such as with the ancient Greeks and Romans

Polygyny a marriage in which a man has multiple wives

Postmodernism a paradigm that holds that human cultural behavior is essentially arbitrary and so can be interpreted in any number of arbitrary ways

Power the ability to force someone do what you want

Prescriptive marriage rules whom you must or should marry

Primitive a term often applied to non-Western peoples, generally with the intent to belittle or dehumanize them (also see savage)

Proactive approach in applied anthropology the idea that anthropological knowledge should be applied when seeking specific change, such as stopping genocide, defending human rights, and the like

Production that part of an economic system in which goods or services are made, so that they can be exchanged and consumed

Project-specific approach in applied anthropology the idea that anthropological knowledge should only be applied to real world situations when there is no other way to avoid impacts to societies by some project

Proscriptive marriage rules whom you cannot marry

Race the idea that humans are divided into specific groups based on certain traits, such as skin color

Rank a formalized status where people hold a specific position in a hierarchy with specific duties and responsibilities, such as in the military

Reciprocity an exchange system in which goods and services are given, to be "repaid" at some later date, either generalized (value or time of repayment not specified, such as a birthday gift) or balanced (value and time of repayment specified)

Redistribution an exchange system in which goods flow into a central place where they are sorted, counted, and reallocated

Religion in general, religion is the belief in supernatural powers, beings, or forces

"a" religion a coherent set of specific beliefs about the supernatural, including an explanation of the world (cosmology), and is based on faith

Resource something used by an organism, may be either renewable or nonrenewable

Revitalization movement measures undertaken to reinvigorate a culture, may have a religious component

Rites of passage rituals involved in the transition from one state to another, such as unmarried to married

Ritual culturally prescribed symbolic acts, ceremonies, or procedures designed to guide members of a community

Sanction a penalty for an infraction

Savage a term often applied to non-Western peoples, generally with the intent to belittle or dehumanize them (also see primitive)

Scarification a body alteration in which the flesh is burned (branded) to create scar tissue in some pattern

Science learning new things, either empirically or non-empirically

Sedentary living in one place all the time

Serial monogamy a marriage form, whereby an individual marries or lives with a series of partners in succession

Sex the reproductive morphology of an individual, either male, female, or intersexual.

Shaman a person, typically in a small-scale society, who is the part-time religious specialist, may control the supernatural, and utilize a hidden reality of supernatural beings and powers in order to acquire knowledge, power, and to help others. Commonly is also the medical practitioner

Slash-and-burn a horticultural technique involving the cutting, drying, and burning of natural vegetation from a small plot and planting crops in the field. The field quickly loses its agricultural productivity and another plot must be processed

Society a group of humans that share a common set of traits and (usually) identify themselves as a group separate from other groups

Sociolinguistics the social categories (such as age, sex, gender, ethnicity, religion, class, and even geography) that influence the use and significance of distinctive styles of speech

Sodality organizations based not on kinship but on some common interest, activity, or occupation, such as sororities, fraternities, and clubs

State a level of political complexity in which a society has a large population, complex social and political structures, complex record keeping, urban centers (cities), central authority, monumental architecture, specialization, and the legal control of the use of force

Status one's informal place in a society

Storage taking some resource and saving it for later use

Stratified societies formal and institutionalized inequality, such as class or caste

Structuralism the idea that the structure of social institutions was the key to understanding

Subculture distinctive variations of the primary society. They have some of their own standards and behavior patterns while still sharing common standards with that larger society

Subsistence a complex system that includes resources, technology, social and political organizations, settlement patterns, and all of the other aspects of making a living

Succession patterned, developmental change in a plant community as it evolves to maturity

Sudanese kinship system bilateral, every relative has a separate name

Swidden system a sustainable horticultural system involving the use of slash-and-burn fields but with a planned rotation of those fields over many years

Symbiotic a long-term, dependent relationship between two species

Symbols signs, emblems, and/or other things that represent something in a meaningful way

Syntax the rules or principles of phrase and sentence making

Tattooing a body alteration in a pigment is applied subcutaneously to create an image or symbol

Third World refers to underdeveloped and unaligned states, now mostly developing countries (still in common usage)

Tonal languages languages in which the pitch of a spoken word is an essential part of its pronunciation and meaning

Totem a spirit animal or other entity adopted as an symbol, such as the bear being the totem of the Bear clan

Transgenders a gender category of people that identify themselves different of their biological sex, such as cross-dressers

Transsexuals transgenders who have had their sex surgically changed to match their identified gender

Tribe a level of political complexity in which a society has a relatively large population, a number of settlements, and formal leaders (chiefs) with some actual power

Uniformitarianism the law that the same geologic processes that were active in the past are active today

Unilinear Cultural Evolution the now disproven theory that societies evolved upwards along single line

Unilineal descent descent figured though one side of the family, either the mother (matrilineal) or father (patrilineal)

Value, economic the calculated value of something in an economy; either immediate, diminishing, stable, or increasing

Value, social the general value of something; either subsistence, prestige, or ceremonial

Warfare the organized conflict between two polities, use of force to exert power, includes supernatural warfare

Western scientific method the specific method of empirical research in which data are described, hypotheses formed to explain their relationships, testing is done on the hypotheses and are either supported or rejected, additional data obtained, additional testing, and so forth. Hypotheses must be testable and tests must be repeatable

Worldview the distinctive way a society (or person) sees its place in the world

writing a system of visible or tactile signs used to represent units of language in a systematic way

References

Ackermann, R., S. Athreya, D. Bolnick, A. Fuentes, T. Lasisi, S. H. Lee, S. A. McLean, and R. Nelson. 2019 Association of American Physical Anthropologists (AAPA) Statement on Race and Racism. Available at: https://physanth.org/about/position-statements/aapa-statement-race-andracism-2019/

Albuquerque, Ulysses Paulino, Luiz Vital Fernandes Cruz da Cunha, Reinaldo Farias Paiva De Lucena, and Rômulo Romeu Nóbrega Alves (eds.) 2014 *Methods and Techniques in Ethnobiology and Ethnoecology*. Springer, New York.

Barker, Graeme 2009 *The Agricultural Revolution in Prehistory*. Oxford University Press, Oxford.

Barth, Fredrik 1969 *Ethnic Groups and Boundaries. The Social Organization of Culture Difference*. Universitetsforlaget, Oslo.

Binford, Lewis R. 1971 Mortuary Practices: Their Study and Their Potential. In *Approaches to the Social Dimensions of Mortuary Practices*, edited by James A. Brown, pp. 6–29. Society for American Archaeology, Washington, DC.

Darwin, Charles 1859 *On the Origin of Species by Means of Natural Selection, or the Preservation of Favoured Races in the Struggle for Life*. H. Milford; Oxford University Press, Oxford.

Delgado, Richard, and Jean Stefancic 2017 *Critical Race Theory: An Introduction* (3rd ed.). New York University Press, New York.

Erickson, Pamela I. 2008 *Ethnomedicine*. Waveland Press, Long Grove, Illinois.

Feld, Steven, and Keith Basso (eds.) 1996 *Senses of Place*. School of American Research, Santa Fe, New Mexico.

Galvin, Kathleen A., D. Layne Coppock, and Paul W. Leslie 1994 Diet, Nutrition, and the Pastoral Strategy. In *African Pastoralist Systems: An Integrated Approach*, edited by Elliot Fratkin, Kathleen A. Galvin, and Eric Abella Roth, pp. 113–131. Lynne Rienner, Boulder, Colorado.

Goodell, Jeff 2017 *The Water Will Come: Rising Seas, Sinking Cities and the Remaking of the Civilized World*. Little, Brown, New York.

Goodman, Alan H. 2016 Disease and Dying While Black: How Racism, Not Race, Gets Under the Skin. In *New Directions in Biocultural Anthropology*, edited by Molly K. Zuckerman and Debra L. Martin, pp. 69–87. Wiley, Hoboken, New Jersey.

Gragson, Ted L., and Ben G. Blount (eds.) 1999 *Ethnoecology: Knowledge, Resources, and Rights*. University of Georgia Press, Athens.

Johansson Dahre, Ulf 2017 Searching for a Middle Ground: Anthropologists and the Debate on the Universalism and the Cultural Relativism of Human Rights. *International Journal of Human Rights* 21(5): 611–628.

Jurmain, Robert, Lynn Kilgore, Wenda Trevathan, Russel L. Ciochon and Eric J. Bartelink 2018 *Introduction to Physical Anthropology* (15th ed.). Cengage Learning, New York.

Kavanagh, Patrick H., Bruno Vilela, Hannah J. Haynie, Ty Tuff, Matheus Lima-Ribeiro, Russell D. Gray, Carlos A. Botero, and Michael C. Gavin 2018 Hindcasting Global Population Densities Reveals Forces Enabling the Origin of Agriculture. *Nature Human Behaviour* 2(7): 478–484.

Kelly, Robert L. 1995 *The Foraging Spectrum: Diversity in Hunter-Gatherer Lifeways*. Smithsonian Institution Press, Washington, DC.

Laird, Sarah A. (ed.) 2002 *Biodiversity and Traditional Knowledge: Equitable Partnerships in Practice*. Earthscan, London.

Lang, Sabine 1998 *Men as Women, Women as Men: Changer Gender in Native American Cultures*. University of Texas Press, Austin.

Lewin, Ellen, and Leni M. Silverstein (eds.) 2016 *Mapping Feminist Anthropology in the Twenty-First Century*. Rutgers University Press, New Brunswick, pp.41–64.

Mascia-Lees, Frances E., and Nancy Johnson Black 2017 *Gender and Anthropology*. Waveland Press, Long Grove, Illinois.

Morgan, Lewis H. 1851 *League of the Ho-dé-no-sau-nee, Iroquois*. Sage & Brother, Rochester, New York.

Myers, Fred, and Nicolas Peterson 2016 *Experiments in Self-Determination: Histories of the Outstation Movement in Australia*. Australian National University Press, Canberra.

Neely, Sharlotte, and Douglas W. Hume (eds.) 2020 *Native Nations: The Survival of Fourth World Peoples* (3rd ed.). Charlton Publishing, Vernon, British Columbia, Canada.

Ottenheimer, Harriet Joseph, and Judith M. S. Pine 2018 *The Anthropology of Language: An Introduction to Linguistic Anthropology.* Cengage Learning, Boston.

Palinkas, Lawrence A. 2020 *Global Climate Change, Population Displacement, and Public Health: The Next Wave of Migration.* Springer Nature, Switzerland.

Posey, Darrell Addison 2001 Intellectual Property Rights and the Sacred Balance: Some Spiritual Consequences from the Commercialization of Traditional Resources. In *Indigenous Traditions and Ecology: The Interbeing of Cosmology and Community*, edited by John A. Grom, pp. 3–23. Harvard University Press, Cambridge.

Rappaport, Roy A. 1971 The Sacred in Human Evolution. *Annual Review of Ecology and Systematics* 2: 23–44.

——— 1999 *Ritual and Religion in the Making of Humanity.* Yale University Press, New Haven, Connecticut.

Service, Elman R. 1962 *Primitive Social Organization: An Evolutionary Perspective.* Random House, New York.

Stein, Rebecca, and Philip L. Stein 2017 *The Anthropology of Religion, Magic, and Witchcraft* (4th ed.). Taylor & Francis, New York.

Sutton, Mark Q. 2017 Voices from the Past: Conceptualizing a "Fifth World." *Journal of Anthropology and Archaeology* 5(1): 17–19.

——— 2021a *Archaeology: The Science of the Human Past* (6th ed.). Routledge, New York.

——— 2021b *Bioarchaeology: An Introduction to the Archaeology and Anthropology of the Dead.* Routledge, London.

Sutton, Mark Q., and E. N. Anderson 2014 *Introduction to Cultural Ecology* (3rd ed.). AltaMira Press, Lanham, Maryland.

Tyrre, Ian 2013 The Myth(s) that will not Die. In *National Myths: Constructed Pasts, Contested Presents*, edited by Gérard Bouchard, pp. 46–64. Routledge, London.

Williams, Walter L. 1986 *The Spirit and the Flesh: Sexual Diversity in American Indian Culture.* Beacon Press, Boston, Massachusetts.

Index

For Product Safety Concerns and Information please contact our EU
representative GPSR@taylorandfrancis.com
Taylor & Francis Verlag GmbH, Kaufingerstraße 24, 80331 München, Germany

www.ingramcontent.com/pod-product-compliance
Lightning Source LLC
Chambersburg PA
CBHW070343270326
41926CB00017B/3961

www.ingramcontent.com/pod-product-compliance
Lightning Source LLC
Chambersburg PA
CBHW070336270326
41926CB00017B/3882